# KONG DAY

QUANTIFYING YOUR
LIFE TO SUCCESS

TOM WATSON MSc

Cover image by: U.T, 99Designs
Book design by: SWATT Books Ltd

Printed in the United Kingdom
First Printing, 2022

ISBN: 978-1-7392382-0-9 (Paperback)
ISBN: 978-1-7392382-1-6 (eBook)

Kongday Ltd
Southampton, England

www.kongday.com

# CONTENTS

# INTRODUCTION

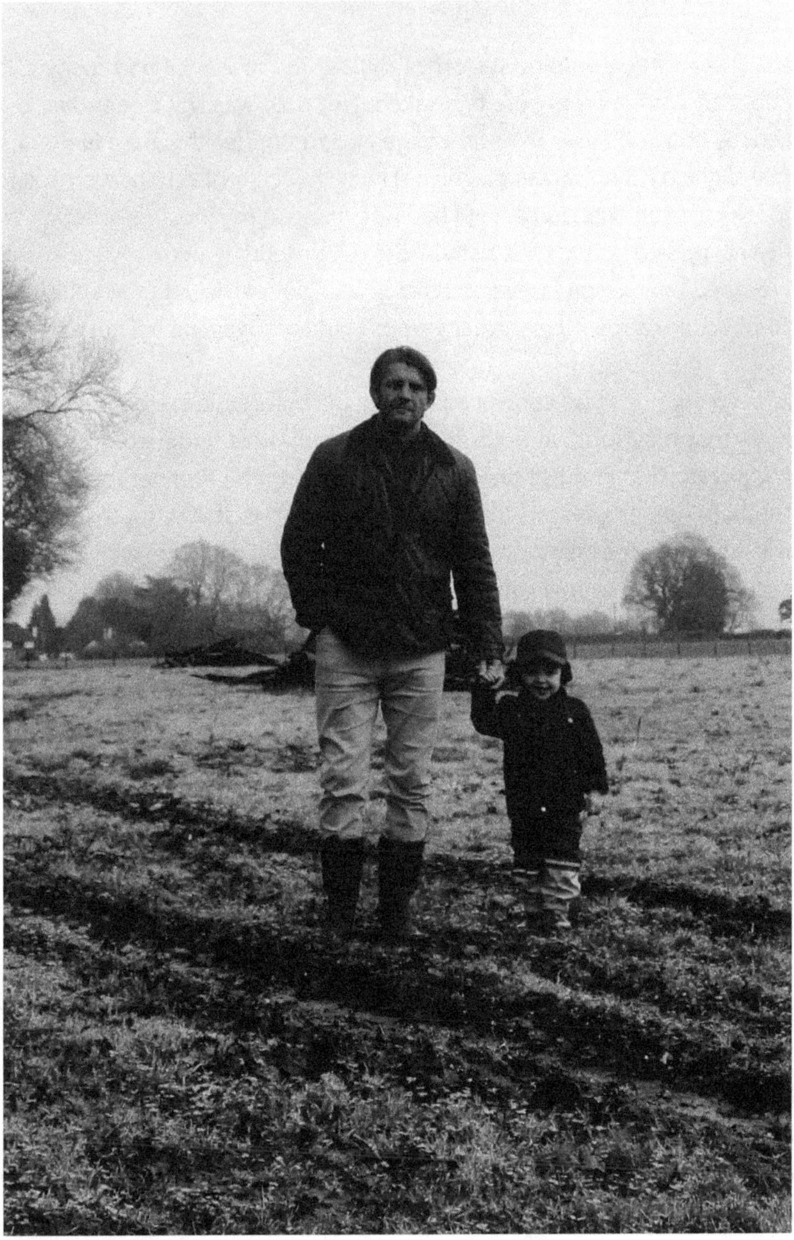

# A turning point

AS I LEFT the neurologist's office in Brighton in 2019, I had many questions about the direction my life had taken. Not only was my career over but I had serious concerns over my immediate and future health. Like a lifelong smoker that is given a lung cancer diagnosis I knew my current actions were responsible for these health concerns, yet I had not changed my life. The emotion weighed heavily upon me, and I felt a strange urge to meditate upon my life and its path. I recalled how despite never practicing a single martial art until adulthood I had climbed to the top 20 in the dangerous world of cage fighting, but why and how?

As a young boy I was convinced I would play professional football. Most young boys that play football hold this dream, but I was under contract at Reading FC, a team that in those times was approaching the Premier League of English football. As I progressed through school with this status, football seemed like my future and destiny. Upon becoming released at the final stages before securing a professional contract I was smacked in the face with the reality that I was not good enough. Looking back, I could see that I had struggled to deal with the internal disappointment of not becoming a footballer more than I ever let on to others or myself at the time. I now left the neurologist's office in tears in a similar predicament. Fighting had really become a way to fight back to those who had declared me as not good enough, albeit in a different sport, and now I was suffering the health consequences. The ego boost and masculinity that had defined my life to become a champion fighter was now a cause for sadness. The trophies, belts and accolades were long gone; no one feels sorry for the smoker dying of cancer.

Looking further back I began to self-reflect on the why. I had grown up in a farming family and a countryside school that depicted a quintessential English countryside as a perfect environment to raise a boy. Deep at the core of my upbringing I saw a man's respect for the tough, fighting man. Many traveling families and members of the town developed a clear marveling and respect at a person's ability to be the tough guy. Despite technology now changing school dynamics, the physically dominant often still hold positions of power and get the admiration of the opposite sex. My strange path into the world of nightclub bouncer and fighting champion brought admiration and respect from random strangers I had never even met. I could reflect back to many one-night stands where I had not even gotten a name. This subconscious need for fake validation from others was the root cause of my health demise because I was trying to please people I did not know.

You see, as a fighter you can choose to compete defensively and take minimal damage in a strategic, technical battle. This is where the comparison to chess in boxing comes from. If you watch any of my pre-UFC (Ultimate Fighting Championship) fights this minimal contact style was more often the norm. I would look to move, dancing and floating around the cage to win technically, often not even taking a single hit. Once I reached the pinnacle of the UFC it was a different story, as I switched to imitating a 'lock stock' brawling style that meant I intentionally took hits purely to please the crowd. You read that correctly – I have been in many fights against the best in the world and dropped my hands to give them a free punch. Stupidity at its finest, my alter ego and marketing persona had damaged the real, unseen me.

Most who meet me will comment how different my quiet, softly spoken demeanour is to the fighting man they had watched over the years. This made the tears worse on that day in 2019. Who would be there to support me financially for the tough times ahead. Who would be the family provider once the neurological demise kicked in? With a 1-year-old son who was going to be the one needing care and looking after? Where were the people who had raved about this style now? I had given my blood, body and brain damage directly for their entertainment. Why were they not here, queuing up to contribute to paying for ways to fix the state of my health? This was the first lesson I learnt:

*Spend more time understanding yourself.*

This was the first time ever in my life I had sat meditating deeply about me. I had wasted my entire life trying to please other people. I wish I had done this earlier in my life after or perhaps even before my football dream was shattered. How many other people had their own similar internal chaos that they ignored? I urge anyone reading this book to pause and open up a period of time that forces you to look deeply at life and your own direction and history. Most will only reach this stage when the deathbed or diagnosis makes change too late.

# Some key questions

This ultimately brought me to understand what any future time I had left on the planet should be focused upon. I had spent my life at the upper levels of elite performance and knew how to improve metrics for world level success. I knew how to organise routines and manage both time and money. If I could figure out a way to improve my health and life experience, how could I use that to help others find their own upgrade in life?

Drumroll fades out as I introduce my system, The KongDay System:

*What have you done with your time?*

This question is your first mission and troop calling. Only once you have a grasp on this should you move to the next question:

*What would you have liked to have done with that time?*

Both these questions put under scrutiny the skills that a person possesses (or wants to). The skills you have developed are the product of your actions over time. Nothing can change your past but that is your reality. Any future time is your opportunity to change and create a different meaning to your limited time on the planet.

I have found since working with numerous clients that most people feel perplexed in trying to produce answers about meaning and their life. Finding those answers is a key part of the KongDay System, as you will see.

The skills I had acquired meant that I could teach people how to fight, but was there a use for that in modern society? After some careful thought and preparation, it turns out that there is. I now work with the police and many industries in teaching self-defense, via a community interest company called ACT. We aim to bring all the benefits of martial arts without the need for dangerous contact.

Further, I have found that I had an ability to give people the confidence to make real change to their lives. I made my way in an industry that only respects struggle. Race, wealth or privilege count for nothing to make it to the top. I had spent my life traveling the world, where turning up somewhere new meant that people had no knowledge of who you were as a person. As Leonardo Di Caprio declares in the movie *Catch Me if You Can*, "People only know what you tell them". Like the story's (true-life) protagonist Frank Abagnale Jr, I was proof that you can fake it till you make it. Faking it might sound like the wrong choice of wording to some but to me it represents belief. Belief is very hard to have when you start out in an area with poor skills. I had learnt that limitations are only truly defined by our internal voices, and this became my conclusion about my skill set that could really help others. I was able to dismantle a damning doctor's office breakdown and career-ending verdict to finding meaning. My life meant I had learned to keep going until the belief is no longer fake. Imagine being told right now that you can never ever again do what you do right now for money. What are you going to do? Due to spending decades in combat, I had learned to become very good at controlling and silencing the inner panic voice. This has become a key strength I have passed to others. You choose your attitude to life and need to continually reinforce the skill to do this.

> *"Everything can be taken from a man but one thing: the last of the human freedoms — to choose one's attitude in any given set of circumstances, to choose one's own way".*
>
> Victor E. Frankl

My clients implement small manageable sufferings (such as fasting, breath holds or physical challenges) to master their stress levels and daily discipline. Just because you were a champion yesterday, your actions today will make the champion of tomorrow.

*I had my life answer.*

Time is the most valuable metric we will ever get yet, none of us respect it. I wanted to teach people how to master their time so that at whatever point they died they would have the satisfaction, that they could not have gotten more out of their journey. We all have completely different circumstances and wants or needs. Use my system to find your way.

Fast forward to three years after my diagnosis, to the point of this book. I have completed a master's degree in Peak Performance and devised a system that has made my life better than it has ever been. I now have a system that means, every single day, through quantification, I can see where and how the direction of my time and life is going. I would have not only achieved more if I had used this system earlier but life would have had greater meaning. Heed the cliche and realise it is not too late. The past is gone, that time is no longer you.

# The purpose of this book

This book will find itself in the self-help section in-between far brighter and insightful minds than me, but what system are they teaching to make you the master of your daily time? I cannot teach you how to design rockets, but I can help you to schedule your time and your life so that you will design better rockets and do so with your time focused upon you and your life. And not just rockets! This is the decision I have made: I would attempt to help as many people as possible worldwide to achieve their goals and find happiness while they still have time.

Most of the people that approach me to start consulting do so with a negativity about their own life and skill set. Stop the negativity, simply being able to read this book is a mastery you do not even consider possessing. Skill acquisition simply stops because we all get comfortable. Comfort is why brain cells die. I was comfortable sparring and fighting with others, half of my life had been spent doing it. Failure to challenge and stimulate your brain with new interactions strips neural pathways. There is simply no longer a need to exist.

*So, get out there and create new experiences
and challenges across a host of topics.*

The reason I had retired from fighting was not by choice. I had failed a brain scan and was told that I wouldn't have that many years of good health left to live because of my actions. Aside from my brain, my body was also on its way out. I had endured over 6 major operations in hospital, ranging from both elbows, my back, feet and head. Forecasting the extent of my life expectancy is not going to change or do anything to heal those past actions. Only diligent and consistent work will be sufficient to enable any striving for small gains. Wake up to the fact that death is imminent at any time. Indeed, regardless of whether you die as a young adult or make it to being an elderly member of society, death still occurs, and the timeline lived is short at the end looking back. Failure to recognise this makes you a fool to the reality of time.

*So, wake up now and every single day, start chasing
after what you want to do with your time.*

Every day we miss tiny details that are unique in importance to not only our use of time but the whole causality of you and your behaviours. This book is not preaching for you to live like me. It is a manual for you to lead by your own example. Why not fill your life with days that see you chasing and experimenting with improving in every area possible, that will make life feel better across a host of areas? This system is the first performance suggestion that puts your balanced lifestyle as the true goal.

# The KongDay System

The crux of the KongDay System is built around six founding pillars which currently suggest the greatest evidence towards supporting a healthy life. The system quantifies your actions to work upon these daily:

**SLEEP:** How to improve yours to live longer and happier.

**NUTRITION:** Learning how to create a personalised approach in timing and assessment of food and fluid.

**PHYSICALITY:** Manage your unique vehicle, upgrade it and have a blast because it will one day be idle on the driveway.

**COGNITION:** How to use cognitive actions to enrich your life. Embracing a path of consistency in learning (visual/practical) with the aim of bringing beauty through knowledge into your world.

**RELATIONSHIPS:** Do you need a rallying call for this? Solitary confinement is the supposed worst of all conditions. Being alone kills. Without relationships we are nothing. The whole universe is interactions. How to work deeply on the health of your relationships.

**BALANCE:** The key area of balancing all the above areas and controlling the balance of your immune system. Our universe expresses the Goldilocks zone in the creation of exactly the right conditions for us to be here, right now. Just by being here, now, we are all winning odds higher than a lottery payout. We must implement balance in life or increase the probability of future problems arising.

As you move through my system you will see that my goal is for you to become an expert, the master of your time in these six areas. You will search and be open to advice and help from others, but you need to become the master. You control your destiny. A master accepts that they do not know all the answers but keeps working on perfecting their skill no matter how good they become. The journey is endless and each day you start again.

> *"There are people who say you can't experiment. That condemns you to failure."*
>
> Pepe Mujica

# The power of small wins

The well known photo shown above was taken by my former media manager, professional photographer Scott Hirano. Conor McGregor is of course now a global superstar, and this was snapped backstage immediately after losing to Floyd Mayweather in that unique fight in 2017 - the only time two champions, each from the worlds of boxing and UFC, have met in the ring in such a high-profile fight. Despite all the money and fame surrounding the bout, the photo captures McGregor's quiet moment of reflection and love for his family - it is these small moments which are the bedrock of life. When any of us look back at our lives, it is often the intricate and intimate moments that we cherish. In all my fights and championships, the unique journeys that occurred with friends and family/teammates are what I cherish the most.

When McGregor made his UFC debut in 2013 in Sweden, I was the guest fighter paraded to the crowds. I had just won a huge fight in the UFC and received a double bonus for best fight and best knockout, rewarding me with well over 6 figures for minutes of work. I was riding high, and McGregor was an unknown, and yet, as life has panned out, I would not change my life for McGregor's (net worth of $180m per Forbes 2019). This is not a statement to put his life down, as I do not know much about it, but more a celebration of the happiness I have found from working daily on the real areas that improve life. Winning at work is not everything, it is just a small area of your life. Once you embrace your story, your daily actions become small wins. Consistency makes these accumulate and the benefits from them multiply. This is the essence of KongDay, and is what this book sets out to help you to achieve:

*Every day starts with a focus to achieve small wins that over the course of a lifetime produce big results.*

In each of the six areas I will now give you a snapshot example of some small wins you can achieve each day. You will discover how to quantify time periods and lay out the purpose and benefits of making the effort to undertake these and, importantly, monitor and record your progress along the way.

Consider, for example, the following 5 small daily wins, each one contributing in its way to one of 5 key areas:

1. Physicality: Completing a 5-minute stretching mobility routine
2. Nutrition: Avoiding just one food you're trying not to eat
3. Cognition: Reading for 5 minutes
4. Sleep: Endeavouring to gain an extra 15 minutes sleep
5. Relationships: Spending 5 minutes quality time with a friend or family

*Completing all 5 would take up 30 minutes of your day, just 2% of your daily time.*

These are all examples of small wins and yours can be anything you decide. Some choose making the bed as soon as they wake up, others avoiding food late at night. Make a list now below of your own 5 with whatever springs to mind. There are, however, two conditions:

- They should be one from each or the 5 pillars we have talked about, thus achieving the 6th pillar, balance, in their benefits.
- As we're just starting out here, the cumulative time set aside for them should be no more than that same 2% of your 24-hour day, 30 minutes.

1. Physicality:
2. Nutrition:
3. Cognition:
4. Sleep:
5. Relationships:

If you start completing these small wins daily, then, crucially, these become habits and it is changing your habits which start to change your life, often significantly. We will discuss in this book how to delve deeper into each area but here I am getting you to focus on the importance of small wins. The great thing is, they are easy and a great way to start. They will have been of your choosing and are the beginning of you consciously deciding to have some daily targets. Consistency also brings positive change to your character — you know you can rely on sticking to your own word and this is crucial. By hitting your own agreed small targets *consistently*, day after day, the cumulative effect is that you start to change your life and, ultimately, change your character for the better.

*That is the essence of KongDay.*

If you work on completing your 5 total wins for the 30-minute period of an average human lifetime (78 years, taking off 18 years for school-age freedom) it would equal 854,100 minutes or almost 15,000 hours! Remember, this is from 5 small daily wins!

The field of self-help is littered with material to help change, be it changing your habits, physical prowess, losing weight, the list is endless... But there is never any system to monitor our most valuable resource: time. Many people shun the self-help sections in bookshops, taking a negative approach, posing questions such as, "Why would I need to change?" As humans we do not like change, but change is ultimately about progressing and advancing a continual adapting state. All of us are changing daily, and there is evidence of this process. How we eat, live our life, and conduct ourselves in our interactions, are constantly changing.

Q: For a moment, I want you to imagine what superpowers or changes you would make if you had zero limitations. Imagine incredible feats or see yourself doing something impossible. Write this here:

---

In my lifetime of chasing world class sporting performance, I made the top twenty of my second career sport (after striving at football) and achieved numerous world titles despite not practising any martial arts until adulthood. I was not particularly good technically compared to the Olympic champions or martial arts prodigies who competed alongside me at the highest level. How then, was I able to compete successfully at their level and defeat many of them?

The answer was I used an early form of my system to develop an unbreakable mindset. No matter who I competed against I was never broken. I have enacted daily small and large *consistent* actions for decades. I simply became a product of my daily behaviours and approach to managing life. My single greatest skill was how I forged my mind. I went from a scared little boy to a man who was waiting backstage to face some of the greatest fighters in the world and could fall asleep due to suffering minimal pre fight stress. I mastered how to quieten my mind and control my inner voice. In the face of extreme stress, you need to become best friends with the internal voice we all possess. That inner voice is a tricky thing, all too prone to focusing on the negative. All of us have an inner voice which wants to sabotage and bring us down with negativity and doubt. It loves to paint future hypothetical scenarios which illustrate why we should not take a different course of action, as it vividly voices things going wrong before they have. Does this sound familiar?

Only by taking the time to listen to that inner voice, helped by ensuring there was silence all around me, did I train myself to tame it and to turn its negative bias into a positive one. This takes time and training, as we shall discover in the Cognition chapter.

Sadly, I believe that because most of us never actually sit in silence now, we do not listen properly to our inner voice to recognise its potential to bring us down all the time. Only by recognising its power can we undertake the necessary cognitive training to harness this as a force for good in our lives. It has the power to be make or break us! This may sound contradictory, but it is only by quietening your mind that you can find your true voice. Do not run from your voice. Sit in silence and communicate with it.

And yet, all too often we run away from listening to it at all, through a daily dose of constant noise and stimulation, a babble which prevents us from engaging in true communication with ourselves and with others.

Q: So, take a moment now. Close this book, close your eyes and sit in a place of complete silence for roughly five minutes, more if you wish. Do this now before reading on.

Write here what you have experienced:

_____

_____

_____

_____

If you are honest with yourself, what did you hear in your brain? Was it still time spent reminding yourself about future tasks, an email you need to send or something that needs to be done now? Did you find yourself dwelling on negative thoughts? How about, instead, taking 5 minutes to think about some positives, for example the relationships that are important to your life today?

At its core the messages from the brain will be all about you. Who you are and who the brain wants to dictate to you that you are. I have become a master of shutting this voice down, to then experience silent periods with less and less noise, yet I still need to keep training this every day. The opponent is relentless and will never give up and life will feed the voice with ever more powerful ammunition. We need to become comfortable with conversations with our internal voice by creating daily meditative periods and recording that inner voice. Methods should be used such as setting up daily journalling alongside your system monitoring. I have built a system that has to be numerical (more on this later) because as I learnt in performance, if you cannot quantify things, what results do you even have?

I want to show you my KongDay System and empower you with the consistency to get up every day with drive and passion. Establishing daily habits in key areas will increase your chance of future success and of leading a satisfied life. Consider the celebrities who make the headlines for broken relationships, jail time and depression. They are often the highest achievers in their field, but their lives have been derailed. I have spoken of how I was a master of quietness in mind but my balance at that stage of my life was appalling. I chased after performance goals and neglected relationships and cognition. Beware of the perils of a one track driven mind. I do not want, after receiving my masters in Peak Performance, to encourage people to go down that singular path. Simply chasing peak performance is, to be honest, easy. Chasing peak performance while leveling up your feelings and balancing your entire life is hard if you do not quantify your actions. Achieving the crucial balance you need is difficult. We all want life to be better, but wanting, on its own, doesn't cut it.

I will repeat I was a champion and achieved what I set out to accomplish but what was the point without placing regard to other key areas of my life? Despite no opponent ever breaking me or knocking me out in well over 100 fights, many parts of the rest of my life were broken. No championships or wealth achieved will fix that. I have to keep working on being focused every day to ensure I do not suffer future regret.

_____

_____

_____

_____

# The six pillars of KongDay

The System is simple and designed upon the key variables that affect a person's life. These are the six pillars I mentioned earlier:

- Sleep
- Relationships
- Balance
- Physicality
- Nutrition
- Cognition

I have reordered these from how I first introduced them, using the first letter of each area to develop a simple acronym that becomes important to be etched into your mind:

- START
- RECORDING
- BECAUSE
- PROGRESS
- NEEDS
- CONSISTENCY

The success of the System depends on you recording and documenting your actions. Your quantifying system becomes more accurate and a stronger indicator of where to focus the more data you add daily about your actions. Until you achieve consistency and make the areas your daily habits you will never be able to make steady progress. Recording data is incredibly important for elite athletes – the data provides them with a tool to implement strategies that improve performance. We are using the same methodology for your life. This system is not designed for elite performers – it is for everyone! Spending every night socialising with family and friends might feel great but how does this affect the other areas that make up your life? What habits come from the social environment and culture you reside within? I loved every single minute of my fighting journey due to having a clear focus to be the best I could in a defined, singular goal but, it was not good for life. No matter what you do, the passion and satisfaction you will receive from creating meaning in your life only comes, I believe, from living by a system that records progress in ALL the key areas of your life. Placing balance as your driving goal will help you to discover shape and meaning in your life. Questioning yourself daily about the level of balance in your actions will point you towards where you need to focus to achieve equilibrium. Start producing data that means you can analyse all the key aspects of life just like any successful business would to analyse its complete performance.

Neuroscientist Beau Lotto informs us in his book *Deviate* that, "All humans are delusional." Our world, Lotto says, simply exists of molecules and energy; there is no meaning. It is only our senses which give meaning to anything. This reality should alarm you because regardless of delusion without meaning in your life I'm not sure how happy you can ever be. Therefore,

Q: What is your current meaning in life?

_____

Whatever your goal, or without having a specific one, if you spend each day implementing habits in the key areas of KongDay, your life is focused on balance. The complication to life is the unpredictability of those molecules of energy and randomness which can cause serious problems.

*No matter what you do, you will suffer pain and*
*a complete inability to control fate in your life.*

Your life is already a complete product of your lottery of birth and situation. I do not like the verbalisation of happiness because what can that even ever mean to someone who has lost their family in war or never had one? Perhaps you are currently suffering from a terminal health condition or living a nightmare of having just lost your child. Talking of happiness is then a sick joke but the situation still exists. This has and will happen to many people worldwide in great statistical numbers. This is but a reality of the experience of planet Earth for all organisms so we must learn a protocol that gives us a daily focus no matter what.

The genetic material as you read this book is completely outside of your control. The length of your fingers, your unique response to food types have not been chosen by you. You must find a way to embrace and accept the assets you have been given. As humans we must shape our own meaning and push forward. Choosing to attack and embrace life pays respect to those that had their time and memory is but a mere trace in the stardust. Increase the probability of your future days and look around the world at the many success stories of those who refused to give up.

## Create space for yourself

I began working with a female client during lockdown who stressed consistently that her meaning and experience was all about doing everything she could for her children. Your children, friends or family all have to live their own lives, and no matter what you do they will have their own influences and experiences to which we or others cannot fully control. Her meaning was dominating her view of relationships, resulting in her giving little regard to her physical, cognitive or sleep health. Ironically, ignoring the latter meant she was struggling to be good at her sole meaning and desires.

Why is it fine to care for your children's sleep but not your own?

I have always been amazed at parents that will try and make their children eat vegetables and healthy food but act differently themselves. What message does that send, that you matter and I don't? The quicker we all accept that you are number one, the faster we can start trying to master our emotions and actions. The knock-on effect of taking such an approach is that you become more productive, not only for your goal but to those around you. This female client has since implemented key changes that have not eroded the time she dedicates to her children yet she now has far greater balance and perspective in her life. In feedback, not only is she happier but she can now see that her life will have its own meaning and importance when the kids have grown up.

Q: If you have younger children, what happens when you are no longer needed, and they are older? What do you have left? Using your current situation jot down some thoughts here:

_____

_____

_____

_____

_____

_____

_____

_____

What of the child who witnesses a parent who is able to lead a balanced and fulfilled life? Is that not one of the best approaches you can take, to raising your children by being an exemplary role model who is physically robust, eats healthily, is cognitively sharp, places importance on good sleep, and has achieved a balanced mental state? This might sound like a super parent, too good to be true, but truly ask yourself why this can't be the case.

Given this is my book and story, I can tell you that my life has been far from exemplary. I've smashed up cars, badly hurt friends, lost most of my money, been neurologically diagnosed as a concern for brain health, stolen, been in trouble with the law, taken drugs, spent multiple periods in hospital (including for weeks as a child, informed I would never walk again with perthes disease); cheated and yet the accumulation of these moments has made me, me. You have to learn and learning comes from doing. My father always told me as a child that it doesn't matter what anyone tells you, you only learn by doing it yourself. Despite this sketchy sounding list, my life has been one of great privilege and my start in life has been better than that for 99% of the world. What difference does any of the past make to what you can do today, right now anyhow if you don't give the past the power it craves?

I cannot write here about *what you are feeling or have experienced* because your life has been different. Cross out Kong and enter your own monikor before Day. This a the front cover. Make the system powerful to your appellation of meaning.

The bane of social media now is its power effect to making others feel they want (or need) a different life. It is a window onto a constant comparison with others – the grass is greener for that other person, look what they have and did today. Where you went to school, the house(s) you grew up in, the important people that shaped your journey cannot be changed. So, own you and get to creating your future legacy to yourself.

# 1: KONGDAY, EVERY DAY

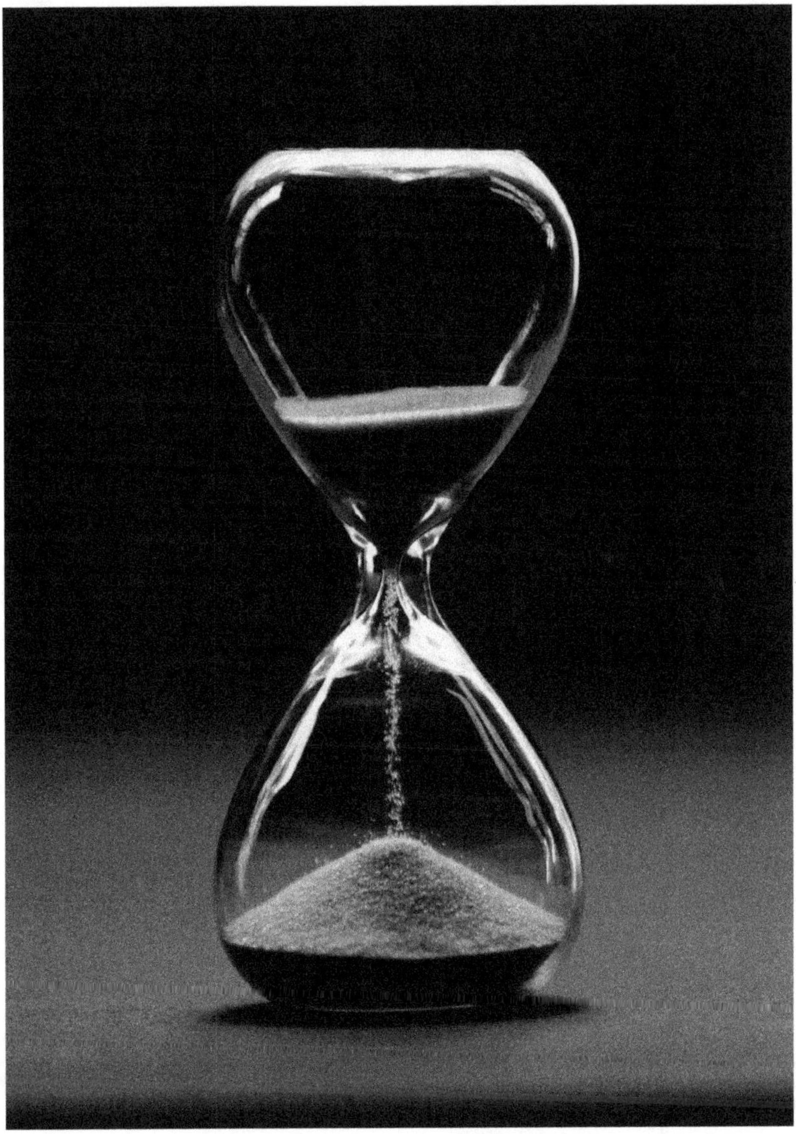

YOUR UNIQUE PATH has led you to the version of you right now. This past can define your future but to a much smaller degree than your future potential will if you get to work now, no matter your age or situation. We can all tackle the future. And for this I have created a KongDay daily mantra defined as:

*Every day, be 6.3% Gorilla*

I was Kong the fighter and we are 99% similar to apes in our DNA and 6.3% is 90 minutes of your daily time. If you want the probability of your future life to look better you need to guarantee that every single day, separate from your 2% small wins already outlined, you will get up and ensure that 90 minutes will be spent on balancing the following KongDay areas, regardless of your life goals or situation:

- Physicality
- Cognition
- Relationships

Progress Cannot Rest

And then add in these two essential ingredients too:

- Nutrition
- Sleep

You need to focus equally on these 5 elements, in other words you need a balance of focus between all of them. In turn, by doing so, you will achieve a wider sort of balance, that of every aspect of your life.

# How can I be 6.3% Gorilla?

In the Introduction I showed how easy it is to find 30 minutes, or 2% of your day, to make daily incremental improvements to the key areas of your life. 30 minutes is a great start-point, but, in my experience, and that of dozens of my clients, the optimum amount of time to set aside for cultivating daily habits is 90 minutes, or 6.3% of each day.

# Breaking down the 90 minutes

Make a start by reading a book for 20 minutes to satisfy some of your cognitive score, T-minus 70 minutes.

Workout physically for 20 minutes, T-minus 50 left.

Focus on your nutrition by spending 10 minutes planning some healthier meals.

Dedicate 20 minutes with no distractions to talking to your partner or members of your family, to enhance the health of your relationships.

Set the alarm 20 minutes later than usual to gain a little more quality sleep. You get the idea.

*Objective achieved.*

6.3% is a paltry amount of your daily time. If you want to work on today and the future, truly commit to at least hitting 90 minutes every single day in the 5 crucial areas. No matter how hard it seems at the start you can get there. Maybe you can only find 30 minutes per day in starting your KongDay journey. 2.1% gorilla is still better than 0%. But remember that would be a small win window of daily time. We are pushing for bigger actions to equal bigger change.

*Just commit. Start small and keep working.*

Within a few months you should be up to hitting your 90 minutes every single day. You will figure out the best way to do this as your journey progresses. Start now with how you intend to attack each area daily and for how long to meet 90 minutes:

**PHYSICALITY**

_____

_____

_____

**COGNITION**

_____

_____

_____

**RELATIONSHIPS**

_____

_____

_____

**NUTRITION**

_____

_____

_____

SLEEP

_____

_____

_____

The area of **balance** is the summary of these actions – balancing appropriately the amount of time you spend on each. For example, spending 90 minutes each day just on a workout, hoping that everything else will improve on the back of this, believe me, that doesn't work.

Remember, the human mind is set up to bring us down. It simply enjoys it, some brains more than others. Only the 6.3% Gorilla learns to quieten the negative mind. It will never completely disappear, but daily consistent action is your fight to silence the negative mind.

I may no longer be a world class athlete, but I still want my life to get better. I cannot just wake up daily and sit back hoping fate deals me a good hand. I need to take matters into my own hands and force the future me with consistent work. By doing this I give myself a better chance of future prosperity.

*It is simple. Do not overcomplicate this.*

We all have the same 1,440 minutes per day until we die, no matter what age or situation we have. That's 525,600 minutes per year, or 42 million of them across an eighty-year lifespan, if you really want a mindboggling figure. This is our equaliser. While we can do little to affect what challenges life will present, the earlier we learn it is our responsibility to manage our time, the more we can improve and pack more experience into life. You are the only person controlling the key variable you can control: YOU. The events outside of your control are exactly that, outside. So, leave them there and focus on what can be conquered as I was featured in a advertisement for Sports Direct.

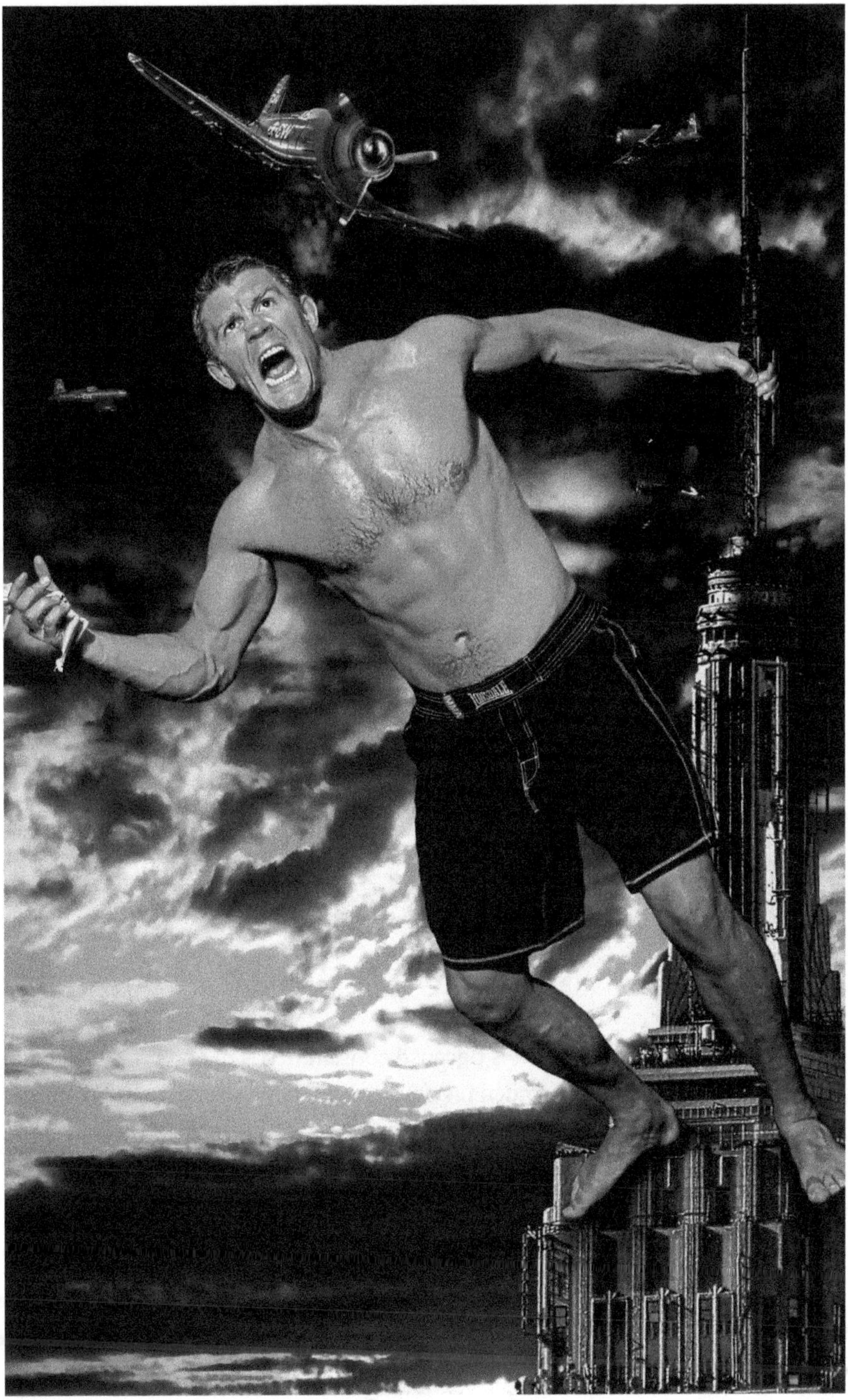

# What gets measured gets done

Start by asking yourself a couple of questions and noting down the answers.

Q: What have your habits and actions been today or for the last week?

_____

_____

_____

Look at your above answer and write down in clear quantifiable percentages
how much time you spent performing these habits:

_____

_____

_____

_____

If this exercise was a struggle, it is because consistency is our biggest challenge, and so we are guessing how much time we spend doing things daily. You brush your teeth every single day at least once or twice without fail so this is a habit we can quantify. If you spent 5 minutes of your day cleaning those teeth it equals 0.0035% of your daily time, although it's probably less, you have your quantifiable daily action. Move your whole life onto this method of thought and you become aware of how your time is spent.

Now, please do not panic. This will become a simple method, not robotic, laborious and time-consuming. If I challenged you to master Russian in two minutes a day you would probably argue that it would be pointless and do nothing for mastery. But when challenged to spend longer periods of time each day, most people immediately declare that their lifestyle does not allow such luxury. Learning 2 minutes every day for a year would mean allocating 730 minutes which is just over 12 hours. That did not take long to work out. 12 hours is on the journey to mastery, not to mention where you might be if you performed 5, 10 minutes or longer timeframes. Take regular simple notes in this journal to help you reassess and quantify your exact periods of time spent. This book, with its spaces to answer questions and make notes, is designed to help you to start the journalling process, but to make it more of a daily habit, equip yourself with a notebook/diary in which to make regular entries. Do you think you would be better at Russian if you spent a year practising the above method or spend 12 hours one day of the year learning Russian?

Consistency is key, no matter how small.

## KongDay schematic

The schematic below is something that I have found useful for clients to refer back to and see the interaction between areas. At the core of everything will be your values and your unique history. As you progress, through committing to taking regular actions, your outlook and values will likely evolve, meaning less preference is given to troubling past memories. Journalling is a direct, practical tool extending from this field and must be used. Making notes in this book is a quick tool but as you progress you need to make more comprehensive notes, on your computer using spreadsheets (more about these later), creating a bedside journal and using any other additional tools you find helpful.

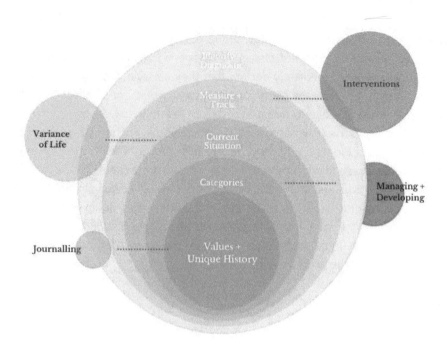

# Identify a baseline

We need to begin to establish a baseline of how you currently score in each KongDay category. Identify where you are and where you want to go in your life. In this first stage it is crucial to work hard on finding your current *KongDay Daily Score*. This score gives you a clear and concise position from which to decide which area you need to start giving priority towards.

Q: Without analysis, score yourself out of 5 how you think you currently score in the following areas daily:

Sleep: _____

Relationships: _____

Balance: _____

Physicality: _____

Nutrition: _____

Cognition: _____

Does anything stand out? Next to these scores I would like you to write a score of what you would rate each area of your life so far up to this point. Does this change your scores?

Both scores will be important for deciding your priority for future interventions and strategies.

## Using a diagnostic tool

To now create an accurate baseline, we must collate as much data as possible to properly analyse our current levels. I might have slept well last night for 9 hours but what if the next 3 days are poor? We therefore need to ensure we have longer term data. Begin with a time period of a week to find your average scores and keep increasing your data set. Find patterns that exist in your sleep, nutrition, relationships, cognitive and physical behaviours around your working week. For example, do you sleep better on certain days?

Take working out but only doing so at weekends. In this case you might show a daily physicality score of 5/5 for those two days and believe your physicality habits are sufficient, perhaps even optimal. If, however, we add in the patterns from the remainder of the week (which sees Mondays scoring a 2/5 and the remaining weekdays scoring 1/5) the average is severely dragged down. Your weekend workouts and a 'mobility Monday' do not even give you 50% of the week's optimal behaviours. You are now scoring a weekly physicality total of 11/35 which is not what could be defined as healthy in the short or long term. Suddenly, the two major physical HIIT workouts you perform at weekends to align with governmental guidance to perform 150 minutes of weekly physical exercise seem poor.

*What we are looking for is daily,*
*consistent habit formation.*

So, using this example of a pattern of physical exercise, I want to encourage you to simply move more frequently. You will learn how to best manage your physical intensity through heart rate variability readings (discussed in depth later in the book). If a heart rate variability is sympathetically high, showing that the immune system needs a rest, then performing intense physical exercise is the opposite of what you should be doing to gain a high physicality score. Without the data to measure your immune system you are just randomly choosing which days to push hard. It is complete guesswork and anything but optimal for health or physicality.

We will now explore each area in detail so that you can fully understand the key concepts, and then move back to the schematic and see how to measure and track your actions in these areas.

# Creating a simple monitor of progress

At the end of each chapter, I have included my personal scoring data from the year 2020. I arrived at this by using a simple spreadsheet program and entering the 1-5 scoring I have mentioned above, to work out patterns and averages. If you do not feel comfortable using a spreadsheet, simply use paper and a visual chart in your home or the free template included at the back of this book. You will be amazed at the patterns you notice about your life once you monitor your daily score over different time ranges. I have chosen to use my 2020 scores as they reflect a consistent year. I could have used various charts that show continual score improving but how does that help you. I do not need to sell my system with snake oil marketing. Once you start using the system any patterns and trends will help you progress your future actions. Any negative, decreasing scores act as a stark highlight to curb your actions.

Here, as an example, are my charts from 2020 monitoring the area of physicality:

### Physical - Visual Shades

|  | JAN | FEB | MAR | APR | MAY | JUN | JUL | AUG | SEP | OCT | NOV | DEC |
|---|---|---|---|---|---|---|---|---|---|---|---|---|
| 1 | 1 | 3 | 4 | 4 | 5 | 3 | 4 | 2 | 3 | 3 | 3 | 2 |
| 2 | 3 | 2 | 5 | 5 | 2 | 3 | 3 | 2 | 3 | 5 | 2 | 5 |
| 3 | 1 | 3 | 2 | 2 | 3 | 2 | 3 | 3 | 3 | 4 | 3 | 5 |
| 4 | 2 | 4 | 2 | 2 | 4 | 3 | 2 | 3 | 4 | 5 | 2 | 4 |
| 5 | 4 | 2 | 4 | 4 | 3 | 3 | 4 | 3 | 3 | 2 | 4 | 4 |
| 6 | 4 | 3 | 3 | 2 | 4 | 4 | 5 | 3 | 1 | 5 | 4 | 4 |
| 7 | 2 | 3 | 2 | 3 | 2 | 5 | 2 | 4 | 3 | 3 | 2 | 4 |
| 8 | 4 | 5 | 4 | 2 | 5 | 4 | 3 | 2 | 5 | 5 | 5 | 2 |
| 9 | 4 | 3 | 5 | 3 | 3 | 4 | 3 | 5 | 4 | 2 | 4 | 5 |
| 10 | 4 | 4 | 2 | 5 | 2 | 4 | 3 | 4 | 5 | 2 | 2 | 4 |
| 11 | 2 | 3 | 2 | 2 | 4 | 5 | 2 | 4 | 3 | 5 | 5 | 5 |
| 12 | 5 | 3 | 3 | 4 | 4 | 3 | 3 | 3 | 1 | 3 | 5 | 4 |
| 13 | 4 | 5 | 4 | 4 | 5 | 4 | 2 | 3 | 5 | 4 | 5 | 5 |
| 14 | 3 | 4 | 2 | 4 | 4 | 3 | 2 | 5 | 5 | 4 | 2 | 4 |
| 15 | 4 | 2 | 3 | 4 | 5 | 3 | 3 | 5 | 4 | 5 | 3 | 4 |
| 16 | 4 | 3 | 3 | 4 | 2 | 4 | 4 | 5 | 5 | 3 | 5 | 4 |
| 17 | 4 | 3 | 2 | 4 | 2 | 5 | 3 | 5 | 5 | 2 | 3 | 4 |
| 18 | 2 | 2 | 3 | 4 | 5 | 4 | 2 | 3 | 3 | 5 | 5 | 3 |
| 19 | 4 | 4 | 2 | 3 | 3 | 3 | 5 | 3 | 3 | 5 | 5 | 4 |
| 20 | 3 | 1 | 3 | 5 | 3 | 4 | 5 | 4 | 3 | 3 | 5 | 4 |
| 21 | 3 | 3 | 2 | 5 | 3 | 5 | 5 | 5 | 3 | 5 | 3 | 5 |
| 22 | 4 | 1 | 2 | 5 | 3 | 3 | 4 | 4 | 3 | 4 | 2 | 3 |
| 23 | 3 | 3 | 1 | 5 | 2 | 4 | 4 | 5 | 3 | 4 | 5 | 4 |
| 24 | 4 | 4 | 5 | 5 | 3 | 2 | 4 | 2 | 2 | 5 | 5 | 5 |
| 25 | 2 | 4 | 4 | 4 | 3 | 4 | 3 | 4 | 5 | 4 | 5 | 2 |
| 26 | 4 | 3 | 5 | 2 | 3 | 2 | 2 | 4 | 5 | 5 | 4 | 1 |
| 27 | 2 | 3 | 4 | 5 | 5 | 4 | 4 | 3 | 5 | 4 | 3 | 3 |
| 28 | 4 | 3 | 2 | 5 | 2 | 4 | 3 | 4 | 5 | 3 | 2 | 3 |
| 29 | 2 | 4 | 4 | 3 | 4 | 2 | 3 | 1 | 5 | 3 | 3 | 4 |
| 30 | 3 |  | 5 | 4 | 3 | 3 | 3 | 4 | 3 | 5 | 5 | 4 |
| 31 | 2 |  | 2 |  | 5 |  | 5 | 3 |  | 2 |  | 4 |

### Physical - Year Score Count

Score 1: 9
Score 2: 68
Score 3: 104
Score 4: 103
Score 5: 82

### Physical Score Counts

|  | January | February | March | April | May | June | July | August | September | October | November | December | Total |
|---|---|---|---|---|---|---|---|---|---|---|---|---|---|
| Score 5 | 1 | 2 | 5 | 9 | 7 | 4 | 5 | 7 | 11 | 12 | 12 | 7 | 82 |
| Score 4 | 14 | 7 | 7 | 11 | 6 | 12 | 7 | 9 | 3 | 7 | 4 | 16 | 103 |
| Score 3 | 6 | 14 | 6 | 4 | 11 | 10 | 12 | 10 | 13 | 7 | 7 | 4 | 104 |
| Score 2 | 8 | 4 | 12 | 6 | 7 | 4 | 7 | 4 | 1 | 5 | / | 3 | 68 |
| Score 1 | 2 | 2 | 1 | 0 | 0 | 0 | 0 | 1 | 2 | 0 | 0 | 1 | 9 |

I respond well to visual interpretations of data, which is why I have created a colour-coding system to enhance the representation of the raw data. It makes it easier to spot patterns, trends and progress (or lack of it!). This is one of those things which takes a few minutes to set up, but then once you have created the template, it's easy to update day-by-day, and then see monthly and yearly trends.

As you can see, for this example criterion, physicality, I have given myself a rating each day of 1-5 and recorded these on a spreadsheet. The method is the same for each of the different key criteria. I have then ascribed a colour to each score and then shown these in a monthly grid and in an annual summary segmented circle. The biggest problem score is a 1, hence colouring this in red, and the ideal score is a 5, hence this is in a more positive green colour. Then, as the illustration above shows, at a glance I can see my progress through the months of the year, reading the chart columns left to right, and I can see my end of year summary by looking at the segmented circle.

As part of my KongDay 90-minute 6.3% of time, updating my five charts (for sleep, nutrition, physicality, cognition and relationships) takes me only 5 minutes each day and is worth every second in terms of the value of the data it gives me. I know, and so many of the people I work with know this too, that only what gets measured gets done. The greatest aid to self-motivation is seeing progress in those charts!

There is more detail on how to score your KongDay journey in Chapter 8.

# 2: SLEEP

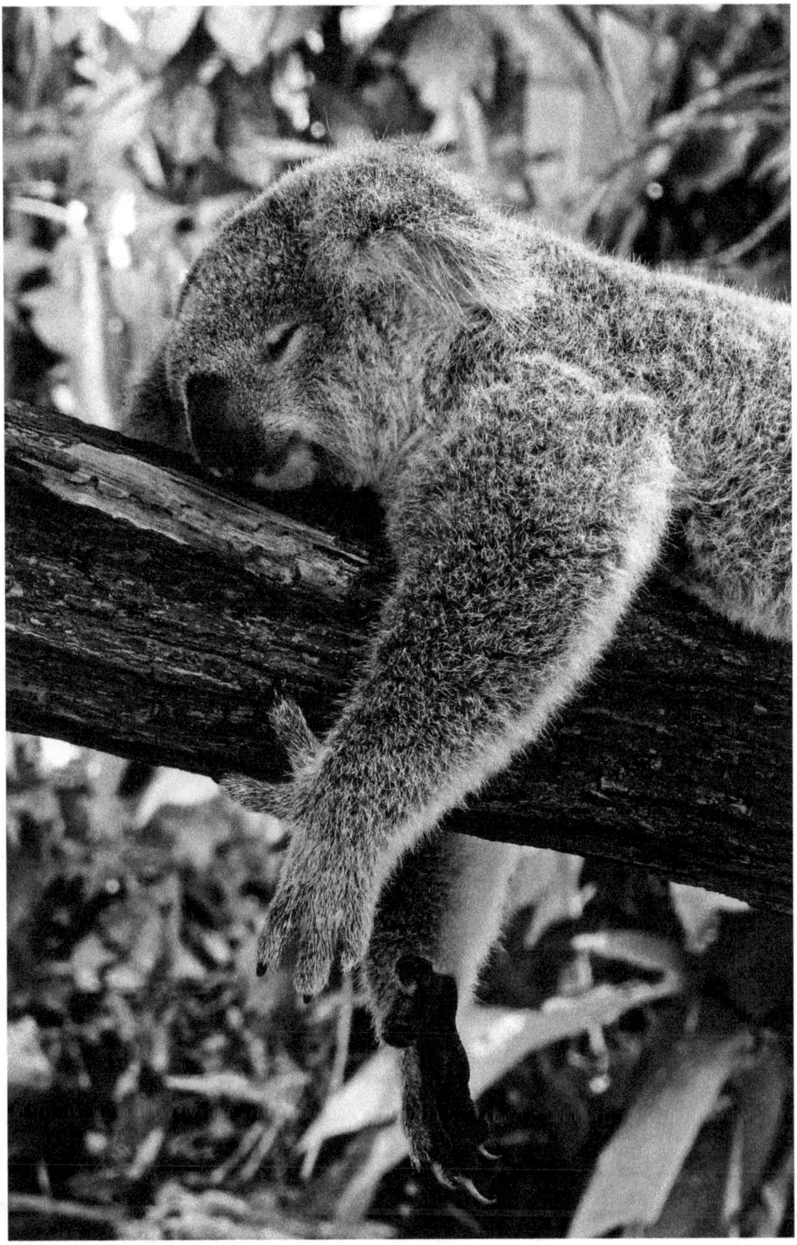

> *"Your future depends on your dreams, so go to sleep."*
>
> Mesut Barazany

WE ALL KNOW how important sleep is. We are bombarded in today's media with how important sleep is for our health, yet this area can be the hardest category to control. Anyone with young children or stress can attest to challenges in not being able to sleep. Our genetics make some of us better sleepers than others but don't let your mind start that excuse running! Indeed, as children we already exhibit natural tendencies on sleep length and sleep type but these facts should not deter us from attempts to get better than our current state.

Q: Do you like to wake up early or stay up late? (This is classed as your chronotype being either an early bird or a night owl).

Your chronotype: _____

Thinking about what you wrote above how do you really know that you are a night owl? Is this because of how your life is set up? Have you ever experimented for longer periods to see if longer terms following opposing chronotype schedules changes your belief?

I pose the above because when I ask these questions to clients, I often find that they have never really experimented with sleep. You may well have spent your whole life up to this point going to bed late in the evening and waking up early. In studies, it has been found that students, who are notorious for staying up late and state they are night owls, perform worse in results than when they sleep and wake earlier. The research demonstrated that when a group of students averaged a late bedtime of 1am, those who went to sleep slightly earlier performed better in next day cognitive testing, despite waking up earlier. Even the readers answering night owls above might benefit from sleeping earlier in improving their daily experience. Of course, context is important but even when I have compared this with (albeit fewer) clients in Spain sleep quality has increased by going to sleep even 15 minutes earlier (consider they also utilised siestas).

I believe that once you start trialing different sleeping methods you will see that conforming to chronotype is overrated. There is a mountain of sleep research out there, but my first message is that no matter what you read, the key action to take is to self-trial various sleep techniques, record the effect, and learn what works best for you. You might be surprised at how complete changes in your sleep regime might open up a different life experience in a positive way.

Sleep is the category which I always encourage new clients to start on and the reason I have made it the first area chapter of explanation in this book. It is such an influential category it makes sense for most people to deal with this first. It is hard to work on cognitive or nutrition improvements when your body is under even minimal sleep deprivation. Any lack of sleep upsets the system and failings can become hard to change until the fog of sleep deprivation is cleared.

The stark reality for why I also encourage trying to master your sleep first is because we spend (hopefully) at least one third of our life asleep (possibly more if you include the extra needed at younger ages). It is therefore hard to comprehend how we cannot be good at sleeping, as we get so much practice at it. I do not think it is acceptable to just keep repeating what you have always done when there is likely to be a better personalised program for you.

In a chance, random meeting I received some advice on sleep from the legendary composer and producer Quincy Jones in California. Jones, notorious for being somewhat of a workaholic and mogul, stated how he had played music with renowned sleep scientist William Dement whilst at university. Jones recounted to me that if I wanted to become as successful as possible then I should dedicate all my focus on sleep if I wanted to achieve greatness. This wasn't just in the suggestion to sleep longer but to figure out how to get better quality sleep in as short a time as possible. He stressed that the time asleep in a lifetime was one third of a lifetime and such a long time to waste in bed! Any way you could shorten this time and not suffer would be extra time opened up to get more done. I then imagined the levels I might achieve on the piano in a 60-year life span if I spent 20 years practising and realised how he had such a mastery of music and entertainment. Forgot 10,000 hours of practice, one third of a lifetime is 20 years, over 175,000 hours! When you see the huge statistics of time spent asleep over a lifetime you might feel like me and decide to just cut down on sleep and spend that time on your life. Many entrepreneurs and cult figures are famed for claiming to thrive on only 3-4 hours' sleep a day because they feel there is so much to do and achieve. However, that, as we shall see, is potentially dangerous talk, particularly when we consider the concept of sleep debt.

## Sleep debt: keep it in context

Sleep debt is exactly as you might guess. It can be defined as the debt you owe for the hours of sleep you have lost compared to what an optimal sleep should have achieved. Worryingly, it has been suggested by sleep scientists such as Matthew Walker to be an irreversible debt, in that no matter what you do you cannot reverse the loss and get it back to boost your account back up. Forget sleeping overtime to get out of sleep debt, our system's damage has been done. Now, I am not a sleep scientist, but the research here contradicts the realities in our life. Clearly, constant sleep debt over months and years cannot be re-credited but it's pointless to focus on trying to claw back hundreds of hours missed due to your past. Plus how many of us have great memories from those late nights of minimal sleep over the year – any trade off would miss these moments.

At the very start of the book, I stated that the past makes us who we are but that we need to discredit and discard a great deal of it. It simply restricts and limits our future. The same is true of sleep debt. Don't worry about the past, just move on to what you can do about tonight's sleep!

## Sleep quantity

Since documenting a mixture of clients and lifestyles I have found that no one I have worked with has benefited from less than 7 hours of time in sleep states. Usually, a sleep state is an hour less that the total time you spent asleep. The extra hour is sufficient to account for waking and movement periods, which makes 8 hours an absolute minimum in bed. If you are experiencing higher physicality, stress or debt then this should probably be closer to 9-10 hours. Basketball legend LeBron James was famous for citing his sleep routine of 12+ hours daily during the full competition season as the key to his success. Personally, if upon waking I notice that I was awake and outside the sleep states for longer than the one hour of awake time, I will adapt my daily schedule to include a buffer by adding a 15-20 min nap to mitigate against some of the sleep debt experienced. No matter what schedule you possess you must prioritise a quick interventional nap if required. Suggesting a difficulty to do otherwise means you still do not currently accept the cruciality of sleep.

In most work situations it is safer and more productive to stop or even to pause and rest for 10 mins over just plowing through fatigue. If circumstances prevent this, there is the option to manage your debt by adding an extra 30 mins to the upcoming night's bedtime. I already hear many readers' voices complaining that this all sounds too easy to achieve. However, look at it the following way. When you make an areas a real priority it is like picking your children up from school, it is not optional.

*You cannot negotiate with your demands — your word needs to be the iron rule to yourself.*

If you want to perform optimally for long periods you need to sleep properly, and all other areas of your life need to fit to your optimal sleep program, not vice versa.

# Sleep cycles

Returning to the advice from Quincy Jones, it is not the amount of sleep you get, it is the type of sleep you gain each night. This is measured by looking at the different stages of sleep, which you can find many clarifications about with a simple internet search. For clients I use the following daily simplification that shows the length of time they should be looking to record if using most wearable methods of sleep tracking.

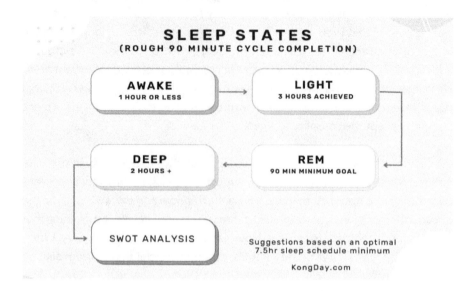

A typical sleep cycle takes 90 minutes to complete, and REM is the area that decreases the most as we age but I set a 90-minute goal regardless of your age. To review your current sleep a SWOT (Strength-Weakness-Opportunities-Threats) analysis is useful to perform to determine where you should place interventional emphasis. This chapter will not be concerned with the full unearthing of current sleep science and states, there are far better and focused books/resources to do this job. We will now focus on wearable options and how they can be integrated to produce useable sleep data.

# Measuring your sleep

I am going to focus on the cost-effective and most accurate method currently available – using a wearable device such as a smart watch (think of the Fitbit or Apple watch as examples).

What these trackers do is take the hassle away from data collection, something which my system is focused upon. You can awake to feedback about your nightly average oxygen saturation levels, breathing regularity or heart rate changes. This data will help to produce a reflection of time in sleep stages and your level of sleep disturbance. If your wearable device does not produce data for your heart rate variability (HRV) score (more on this in the Balance chapter) then I would strongly encourage using a chest strap to measure and record your HRV daily upon waking. You can control light levels for your bedroom and give yourself a simple score on how you feel after waking up. Combining this all together will produce a solid base of personalised sleep assessment.

Your journey to unraveling your unique patterns or behaviours in sleep is much easier using a tracker because you are asleep! The data they produce is coming at a time when you are not functioning on a conscious level. Tracking might show I was in bed for 9 hours last night but only slept for 7 hours. It is very hard to truly gauge restfulness time when sleeping. Sure, you can remember the clear wake times such as when you need to go to the toilet or wake continuously due to noise etc but there are nightly occasions that only sleep state data (shown in heart rate) informs of time you look asleep but actually needs to be classified as restfulness. Without knowledge of my restfulness in tracking I can be convinced I should be sufficiently rested given my 8hr time in bed. We all have days where we think we should feel tired but do not. Likewise, we might sleep for a long time but feel exhausted. Your life and the night's true immune system rest can be picked up by a tracker. I personally only have to eat inside 2 hours before my sleep time to see my HRV rate drop significantly due to the metabolic system working harder than usual (normal optimal eating for sleep would see me stopping food 3-4 hours before sleep).

Working out your best time to sleep and wake daily will help you get the best results and to do this you must try multiple options and evaluate. I have found myself able to avoid stress when I suffer a poor night's sleep due to my young son waking up or social engagements. This is only because I can look at the long-term data and acknowledge or implement ways to reprioritise making up that lost time. I also try to remind myself that one day these moments with my little boy will be long gone so they should be cherished not chastised. Accept what you can't control and just notate the sleep debt. Yes, it is fine to get 4hrs sleep one night and then just carry on as, after all, what can you do about the lack of sleep? Only an acceptance and mitigation plan to try and recover more in the ensuing days is what's left to focus upon.

*Remember, it's not our fault we*
*don't sleep, it's part of living.*

Long-term deprivation is different, and we must accept responsibility and decide we are going to find a change. You need to change your life around to make sure sleep is a key pillar that sets everything else up. If consistently you do not get sleep for months/years you really need to change and put all your focus into solving this problem. If your kids are growing and still not sleeping, this needs more priority than school. What kind of learning will they produce if not? Further, if they don't sleep well, you don't sleep well either. You might be happy to spend thousands on their clubs, learning or family holidays but sleep is worth more!

This was sadly highlighted to me by a client of mine who suffered a stroke in his 40s despite being in tremendous physical shape. It was found that the stroke could largely be attributed to poor sleep and the ensuing stress that this state causes. With four kids he had had to face a period of figuring out how to get everyone more sleep and this meant he was the one left who did not sleep. Take a common side-effect of being a dog owner and experiencing night-time barking. I'm not advocating you put the dog down but paying a trainer or designing them a new sleeping environment no matter the cost is worth it for an issue that might cost you health-damaging events such as a stroke or years off your healthy lifespan.

# Lucid dreaming

Lucid dreaming is the ability to control your dreams. Like me, you may potentially laugh and postulate that you wish such nonsense was feasible. Like me you do this despite having never tried it. In the book *Exploring the World of*

*Lucid Dreaming* by Stephen LeBerge it is stated we can all easily lucid dream by following 2 consistent approaches:

1. Write your recollection of the night's dreams immediately upon waking, in your phone or notebook next to the bed (if you do not always remember your dreams try this anyway as you'll be surprised at how you start remembering more).
2. Perform reality checks. This is done in your waking hours via a simple exercise such as you pinching yourself repeatedly for set periods. Later when dreaming you then try to implement this into your dream. This check helps you realise that you are active in your dream and not awake because no pain is felt from the pinching.

I have found that lucid dreaming starts off as mainly a bit of fun but for some people it can significantly advance their sleep routine. I have had a female client who, having hated going to sleep, transformed into someone who looked forward to sleep because it became like a game where she could attempt to create vivid and exciting experiences. I have conversely had a male athlete that said he would often lucid dream and wished he could stop due to waking up exhausted! These examples highlight the individuality principle and finding your own path. Be creative with your sleep routine and see how changes can help you with your daily scores.

# Dement's Cave

*One of the simplest approaches to better sleep
is to remove light from our bedrooms.*

In the past this was about removing a television but now media devices surround our room with light and stimulation. I've already briefly mentioned renowned sleep scientist William Dement, who founded the Sleep Research Center at

Stanford University. He recommended the number one principle of creating a cave environment for optimal sleep.

So, consider trying to recreate Dement's Cave for your sleep lair. Don't spend much time in your bedroom other than for sleeping. This might sound a little odd, but it will create a subconscious neural pathway that associates the bedroom with sleep and nothing else. If you spend a lot of time in your room other than for sleeping your mind likely associates it less with winding down and simply another social room. Maybe this is why teenagers and young adults that spend all day in their room, struggle to sleep at night. Their brain has a differing association of what a bedroom is.

Blackout blinds are a worthwhile investment but wearing an eye mask will also help. The mask can create a routine for your brain that sleep is due when the habit of putting one on is formed, regardless if it moves during sleep letting light in.

# Too much screentime?

If the world became TV addicts in the 20th century, that is proving to be nothing compared to the screen-time addiction of the 21st century. The UK media regulator Ofcom published research showing that in 2020, UK adults spent a staggering one third of their time watching screen content on TV or online.[1] If this much material is being consumed, no wonder we cannot sleep. Our circadian rhythms are constantly bewildered.

Q: How many hours a day do you browse and watch screen content?

_____

---

1       bbc.co.uk/news/technology-58086629

A surprising insight from KongDay consultations has been the large number of clients contradicting the idea that using technological devices before bed is one of the worst things you can do. I have yet to find many clients who, once a sleep strategy was installed, needed to omit devices right before bed. I feel this is an example of something that makes common sense but might not necessarily apply directly.

Further, I'm not sold that in today's highly technological world that for many shutting down media early is a worthy trade-off. If I want to learn new courses or information, a lot of this now will be via screens. Shutting down this in the evening might help sleep but it creates a limitation on my cognitive input. While the suggestion to disconnect and integrate elements of mindfulness into your routine should be applied, technological disconnection nightly 2-3hrs before bed (as some recommend) doesn't seem a worthwhile use of time. 30 minutes to one hour seems a more sensible approach and the only clear guideline I would enforce is to keep the devices out of the bedroom or add blue light blockers to screens or eyes directly before sleep.

## Increasing REM sleep

Now we have reinforced the essentials of sleep, let's look at REM sleep, the rapid eye movement sleep stage, which research shows to be one of the most beneficial sleep stages.

Currently there is a surge of research trying to define how we can optimise REM state, but with no clear conclusions or recommendations. So, for now, you must become your own sleep scientist. Wearable trackers are quite good at relaying REM stages but the general recommended range is anywhere between 5-50%. Talk about covering the bases! I have found a more realistic range to be 15-25%, with 90 minutes being a minimum goal regardless of age (REM will decrease with age so we want to try to change that). Assessing your hormone levels via a blood test can also be an insightful way to improve REM sleep, by finding nutrients or areas you might be able to supplement to affect sleep (magnesium would be an example). Without delving further into hormonal markers, try adding 30 mins to your sleep and see how this affects your time in REM state. Generally, REM cycles increase the longer you sleep so REM deprived sleepers simply do not sleep enough (REM sleep will also increase heavily the night following a poor night's sleep). How about adding or omitting naps? What about going to sleep at different times and recording the difference or correlations to REM sleep? Always be creative and look for more ways you might be able to trial and question your results before making sudden conclusions about your sleep and health. Once you nail down your REM cycles (as they follow the earlier stages) the other sleep cycles will fall into line.

## Small incremental gains

Research has shown that there are genetic differences in us which can increase or decrease the average amount of sleep we have each night. This equates to plus or minus around 9 minutes per night. 9 mins may not seem a lot but compound that figure and time shows that only one week produces an extra hour of sleep time. The genetically gifted sleepers will get yearly 52 additional hours in bed! This loss or gain is hardwired and so it's not worth fretting about but think about how you could achieve some small gains in your sleep and set about implementing them.

Q: How can you increase your nightly sleep time by 5-10 mins per day?

_____

_____

_____

_____

_____

# The value of napping

Many people can be critical of napping and society often frowns on a nap as lazy and unproductive, but outside of potential worrying signs (napping regularly may be associated with underlying health conditions such as dementia or high blood pressure) cultures such as Spain encourage nationwide siestas with enormous individual and societal benefits.

So, as an intervention strategy it may be an effective and much needed tool. Consider the signs many of us have experienced when driving over-tired, needing to pull over and take a quick stop to refresh. It saves lives by doing so and heavy goods vehicle drivers are bound by UK law to ensure they do not drive over timed limits without taking such a break. I believe that people's focus in implementing napping should be to understand it is not an everyday addition. This would be a sign that you are constantly either overtired or overworked and need a mental break. Like a car that is running low on oil a quick top-up will help complete a journey, but any potential leak still needs to be fixed.

So, if we are going to choose to nap, how? I emphasise to KongDay clients that *a nap should not be taken any later than 8 hrs after waking up* and ideally as early as possible in the period of 6-8hrs after you wake up. This is due to its knock-on effect on your circadian rhythms and ability to sleep at night. Think about the guidance of drinking coffee/alcohol and sleeping. The earlier we can do it, the more time our system has to reset.

In napping it is also important to consider the psychological difference between full sleep and napping. In thinking about what facilitates optimal sleep we conjure images of not being woken by the clock, experiencing a natural waking and rising, but this is the complete opposite for napping. There is a huge risk in oversleeping during a nap. The failure to bring yourself out of napping early means you begin to move through the journey of sleep cycles. To avoid this, set an alarm exactly 10-20 minutes after you start your nap. Regardless of if you fall straight asleep or perhaps have only just drifted off when the timer goes off, at the 10-20-minute mark you must arise. It is also much easier to bracket off a 10-20-minute period, rather than needing to find an hour. Most workers cannot take advantage of lunch breaks or quick opportunities to attack any sleep debt unless a nap is short.

Organisation by the clock is essential to not waste precious time. However, initially it can feel aggravating to set time aside for a nap but then not sleep. This relates to psychology and creating the viewpoint that even without sleeping you can gain similar benefits to those arising from meditation in quieting the mind for rejuvenation. If huge technology companies across Silicon Valley including Google have built nap rooms to increase productivity, then it is worth including napping in your self-testing and day.

The previously mentioned siesta culture in Spain sees 70% of the population stating they don't currently take a nap during the places across Spain where law closes businesses from 2-5pm. I further learnt from my wife that the culture of the siesta is to give you the extra energy to stay up later at night. Spanish culture sees average bedtime hours of midnight or later due to eating late and socialising. Taking an afternoon nap when you sleep at 1am is different from those who go to sleep at 10pm.

I have seen in research papers a suggestion to nap in a slightly upright position, as a tool to avoid the deep sleep states we spoke about avoiding (where I suggested setting a timer), but I don't believe many find this useful. If anything, it just makes it likely that you will not rest. However, if you do not have the luxury to nap lying down then upright is worth an exploration. Anecdotally, I get better results in napping if I drink a coffee immediately before a nap. Upon suggesting this to others I am frequently met by disbelief, but some science supports why this might occur. Caffeine levels in your blood will peak after consuming a coffee at around 40-45 minutes after ingestion. A short 20-min nap window can then coincide perfectly with waking up energised just as the coffee kicks in. Often, coffee consumption might be taken too late to avoid feeling overtired, so note the times you regularly feel lethargic and consider an earlier coffee and/or nap. Also consider the strength of your coffee! A usual amount would have 1.5-2 shots of espresso in it so those consuming higher levels of caffeine might need a different protocol.

So, I hope you have taken onboard the idea that napping, far from being a waste of time, can be an exceptionally good use of time if approached correctly. It can leave you refreshed, energised and ready to approach the rest of your day with extra focus and purpose. And one final thought – if you still can't be convinced to add naps when necessary, try going for a walk, alone, outside and without distraction. This process can act in a similar way to refresh and reset the mind for action.

# Case study: Sleep

Client has worked up to averaging almost 50 hours sleep per week but has a final goal of +55hrs of weekly sleep though monophasic sleeping (one single block).

Difficult for client as has a young daughter who often wakes up at 4am.

Target is 8 hours every night (8x7) = 56 hours. Implement a protocol that every night where less than 8 hours is slept (monitored using tracker) a plan was put in place to increase the hours slept the following day via earlier bedtime or a nap.

Progress towards the target was missed so changed. The first few weeks saw 7 hours on days and often only 6 hours on weekends so missed weekly targets by 3+ hours. New plan was to divide 42/5 creating 8.4 hours of sleep on five days of the week to create a buffer for the failure days.

With the young daughter, the daily wake-up time is usually 6am, creating a major challenge of an early sleep time the previous evening. The target asleep time is therefore 9pm to give a 9-hour sleep window. This entails trying to wind down before sleep and be in bed earlier. This strategy saw client find 2 days a week of 10 hours in bed. The wake-up time never changed. After seven weeks of this regime, 55 hours sleep per week were achieved for two weeks straight with only one nap implemented. New challenge was then presented as client stated that they now felt lazy after achieving goal. This is understandable, as it has meant a big lifestyle change, but ask client to continue for one month and reassess. After this period the benefits of increased rest and resulting improvements in energy and focus make it seem more worthwhile. To help the client assimilate this change, they utilised recommended reading on the book *Rest* by Alex Soojung-

Kim Pang, an excellent framework for shifting the mental concept of rest not being lazy.

Q: What is your current weekly sleep time?

_____

Any consistency of which days are poor/better sleeping days?

_____

# The importance of rest

In the above case study, I used a book recommendation to highlight how a change of belief systems is sometimes useful. We forget that social norms are constantly in flux and can place unnecessary pressures upon ourselves. As Pang succinctly points out in his book, society 100 years ago saw culture striving for leisure and the elites of this time paraded a carefree and relaxing schedule. *This did not mean laziness.* It was determined that intense daily study and concentration was at a maximum period of 3-4 hours. Demanding mental work could not be performed for longer than this (you could argue physical would be similar). Rest became a necessity, spending afternoons in leisure rather than work to ensure the following day could see more deep study.

Today's entrepreneurial societal spirit will spout words such as 'hustle' and 'won't stop', determining sleep as something you do when you're dead. These go-getters may sleep only 3-4 hrs per night and create extra waking hours, but at what price and quality of work? Should we praise someone who doesn't rest or pause in pursuit of goals? Instead, maybe a correctly managed 10 hours of sleep time is far more productive than only sleeping 4 hours. Indeed, my time in high-level sport and business performance demonstrated to me that rest was often the simple key to peak performance. The CEO who is first in and last out is not living in a realistic or sustainable way. The athlete who stays later than everyone else might not be the athlete making the most performance improvements that day. Consider these examples, from people who are in no way considered by history to be slouches:

- Bill Gates takes a week off annually to go to the woods and disconnect from everything, sleeping as long as his body requires.
- Churchill took scheduled naps during the pivotal pressure points of WW2.
- Charles Darwin was well-known for hour-long midday walks to mentally unwind and rest from work.

Q: How can you work smarter not harder?

_____

_____

_____

_____

Let's conclude this section on sleep by underlining its importance, summed up perfectly by sleep scientist Matthew Walker:

> **'Sleeping 5hrs or less can leave you with a heart that looks 10 years older. Sleep = Health Insurance'**
> Matthew Walker

# Key Implementations:
## Sleep

> Create a weekly sleep goal, with defined hours in bed.

> Develop a personalised sleep routine and work on making this a habit.

> Light. Consider the difference of how you feel waking up with summertime light to winter dark. Consider how this could change your sleep needs. Make your bedroom a cave.

> Consistency is key. Don't keep trying to catch up on poor sleep, just be consistent in striving to improve your own sleep routine.

> It is highly unlikely you are getting too much sleep. Increasing your sleep for 5,10,15 mins will slowly pay off regardless of naps or longer sleep nights. Use this with a longer-term target of eventually adding 1 hr per night to your current regime. The rule of 8+ hours is good but is not individualised. Lifestyle may dictate you need more, so begin trialing different timeframes to establish what is your ideal. Think of holidays – you return feeling great but is it solely the holiday or is it your improved mood from better sleep?

> Consider going to sleep well hydrated and upon waking start your hydration early. Change your habit to wait for that morning coffee and sip water before anything else. Finding light early sets off your melatonin and your circadian clock meaning deeper sleep becomes easier later at night.

> Exposure to blue lights before sleeping can create insomnia and bad sleep cycles. Try using blue light or orange tinted sunglasses if you feel affected.

> Schedule naps and see how they work for you.

> Use HRV monitoring to help you to create an effective personalised sleep routine. What are your HRV scores when you wake up at certain times and sleep at certain times? The higher your HRV the better the sleep for you.

> Wake up at the same time every single day, regardless of your chosen blocks. Perhaps you go out late in the evening so decide to sleep an extra hour in the morning. With everyone I have worked with this doesn't help. It just messes up your circadian clock regardless of location. I have found that the time you go to sleep can be less stringent with as little effect as waking time.

> Meditate. Not because it helps you sleep but because it helps you become comfortable with silence and darkness. Going to sleep can be a nightmare for many and it's often because they find it hard to lay still in silence without being uncomfortable. Life is so busy now, with constant stimulation, that it is no surprise the brain feels uncomfortable in silence. The silence acts as a catalyst for our mind to begin racing. You then begin the cycle of finding something to stimulate your mind and create a sleep-damaging cycle, pushing blood pressure and depression levels higher and either avoid the bedroom or lie there stimulated by your phone or screen devices.

> Trial Polyphasic sleeping (sleeping multiple times per day as opposed to just an evening block). I have worked with athletes who sleep 5 hours at night and 3 in the afternoon to ensure greater rest between training sessions.

# My Sleep Score charts for 2020

Sleep - Visual Shades

| | JAN | FEB | MAR | APR | MAY | JUN | JUL | AUG | SEP | OCT | NOV | DEC |
|---|---|---|---|---|---|---|---|---|---|---|---|---|
| 1 | 4 | 2 | 4 | 2 | 5 | 5 | 3 | 3 | 5 | 4 | 5 | 5 |
| 2 | 2 | 5 | 4 | 5 | 5 | 3 | 5 | 1 | 5 | 4 | 5 | 5 |
| 3 | 3 | 3 | 3 | 5 | 4 | 5 | 4 | 4 | 5 | 5 | 5 | 5 |
| 4 | 3 | 5 | 3 | 4 | 5 | 4 | 3 | 4 | 4 | 5 | 5 | 5 |
| 5 | 5 | 4 | 3 | 5 | 3 | 4 | 3 | 5 | 5 | 5 | 5 | 2 |
| 6 | 2 | 5 | 3 | 3 | 3 | 5 | 3 | 4 | 1 | 5 | 5 | 3 |
| 7 | 5 | 4 | 5 | 4 | 4 | 4 | 2 | 4 | 5 | 4 | 5 | 3 |
| 8 | 5 | 3 | 4 | 3 | 5 | 4 | 5 | 4 | 5 | 4 | 2 | 5 |
| 9 | 5 | 4 | 4 | 5 | 4 | 4 | 4 | 5 | 5 | 4 | 3 | 5 |
| 10 | 4 | 2 | 5 | 3 | 3 | 3 | 4 | 5 | 5 | 5 | 5 | 5 |
| 11 | 4 | 4 | 4 | 3 | 4 | 3 | 2 | 4 | 3 | 5 | 5 | 2 |
| 12 | 4 | 3 | 1 | 5 | 4 | 2 | 3 | 4 | 3 | 4 | 4 | 3 |
| 13 | 5 | 4 | 4 | 4 | 5 | 4 | 4 | 4 | 4 | 5 | 3 | 3 |
| 14 | 5 | 4 | 4 | 2 | 3 | 3 | 4 | 4 | 5 | 5 | 5 | 5 |
| 15 | 3 | 5 | 3 | 4 | 4 | 5 | 4 | 4 | 3 | 4 | 5 | 3 |
| 16 | 5 | 2 | 3 | 3 | 5 | 4 | 4 | 4 | 5 | 3 | 4 | 4 |
| 17 | 3 | 4 | 3 | 3 | 5 | 4 | 4 | 5 | 5 | 4 | 4 | 2 |
| 18 | 2 | 3 | 4 | 5 | 5 | 3 | 4 | 4 | 2 | 5 | 5 | 5 |
| 19 | 5 | 5 | 4 | 4 | 2 | 4 | 3 | 3 | 3 | 4 | 5 | 5 |
| 20 | 3 | 5 | 3 | 2 | 4 | 3 | 4 | 4 | 5 | 5 | 5 | 5 |
| 21 | 2 | 5 | 5 | 5 | 2 | 5 | 4 | 4 | 5 | 4 | 2 | 5 |
| 22 | 5 | 5 | 4 | 5 | 2 | 5 | 4 | 3 | 5 | 5 | 5 | 5 |
| 23 | 4 | 4 | 5 | 5 | 3 | 2 | 4 | 4 | 2 | 5 | 3 | 5 |
| 24 | 3 | 4 | 4 | 4 | 3 | 4 | 5 | 3 | 2 | 4 | 2 | 3 |
| 25 | 4 | 4 | 5 | 5 | 3 | 4 | 4 | 5 | 1 | 5 | 3 | 5 |
| 26 | 4 | 4 | 3 | 3 | 4 | 5 | 1 | 3 | 5 | 5 | 4 | 5 |
| 27 | 4 | 3 | 5 | 3 | 4 | 4 | 5 | 4 | 3 | 5 | 5 | 5 |
| 28 | 3 | 4 | 5 | 3 | 3 | 3 | 3 | 4 | 2 | 4 | 4 | 5 |
| 29 | 3 | 4 | 4 | 4 | 1 | 5 | 4 | 5 | 5 | 5 | 3 | 5 |
| 30 | 3 | | 4 | 3 | 1 | 3 | 4 | 2 | 5 | 3 | 5 | 5 |
| 31 | 4 | | 5 | | 5 | | 3 | 5 | | 5 | | 4 |

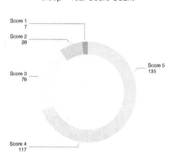

Sleep - Year Score Count

Score 1 — 7
Score 2 — 28
Score 3 — 79
Score 4 — 117
Score 5 — 135

Sleep Score Counts

| | January | February | March | April | May | June | July | August | September | October | November | December | Total |
|---|---|---|---|---|---|---|---|---|---|---|---|---|---|
| Score 5 | 9 | 8 | 9 | 9 | 10 | 7 | 4 | 8 | 17 | 17 | 17 | 20 | 135 |
| Score 4 | 9 | 13 | 13 | 8 | 8 | 13 | 16 | 16 | 2 | 12 | 5 | 2 | 117 |
| Score 3 | 9 | 5 | 8 | 10 | 8 | 8 | 8 | 5 | 5 | 2 | 5 | 6 | 79 |
| Score 2 | 4 | 3 | 0 | 3 | 3 | 2 | 2 | 1 | 4 | 0 | 3 | 3 | 28 |
| Score 1 | 0 | 0 | 1 | 0 | 2 | 0 | 1 | 1 | 2 | 0 | 0 | 0 | 7 |

# 3: NUTRITION

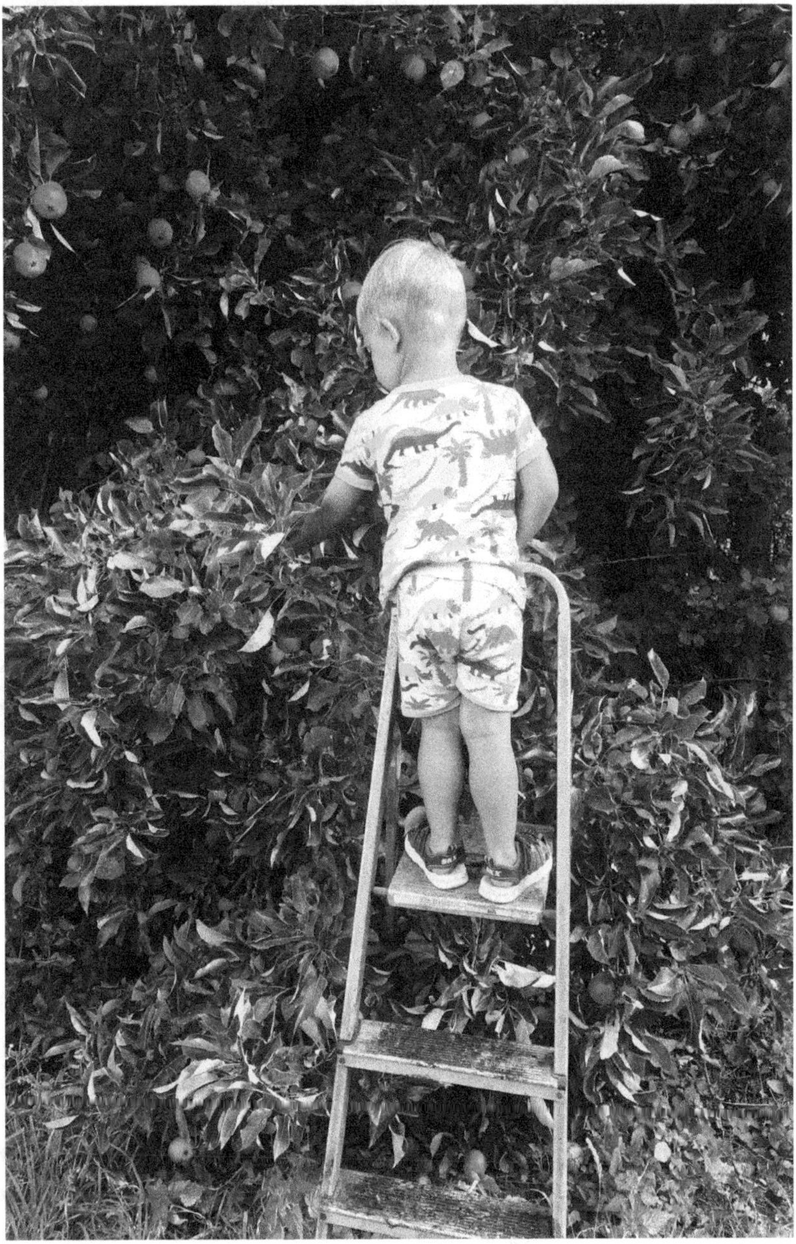

OUR BEST ASSET as human beings has been to learn and pass on wisdom from challenges, to adapt and remodel the future as we wish. This process has led to you, the physical entity that sits reading this book. This brings me to my first nutritional point, often overlooked, which is to look at the nature of eating. We must first acknowledge that without previous guidance and wisdom we would still be at daily risk of death in even trying to figure out what we can eat. So, simple gratitude for that progress is a good start-point which helps a person eat less and more mindfully. Modern agricultural methods currently take a lot of stick but remove them and many of us would be starving, as large parts of the world still experience or those who attempt 100% self-sufficiency. Nutrition is where you will find more pseudoscience and nonsense than in any of the other KongDay categories so this chapter will be concerned with simple truths.

# Unhealthy obsessions

I used to help clients with an initial declaration that there was no definitive right or wrong way to eat. I have since changed my approach because encouraging some maxims such as "everything in moderation" does not help people with their real goal of avoiding certain foods. Many foods while they differ with individual responses (consider an insulin index chart) are far more likely to be a *healthy* choice over others. We want to create your own personalised food consumption strategy that suits and benefits your situation and goals. You need to understand that many foods will not benefit you, no matter what their portion size. If this makes you think that life is not worth living because you cannot have x food, then you should understand you already have an unhealthy attachment to certain foods.

In the past I have forced myself and others to refrain from foods that in fact might be beneficial. Consider something like blueberries or even drinking coffee. Any Google search will support a myriad of health benefits, but can you go without either for a month? Most probably agree with blueberries they could but coffee... regardless of food or drink, anything which you cannot go without is problematic. The greater the addiction the greater the need to omit that substance. Anything you cannot live without is an addiction and therefore an unhealthy relationship. We might love apples over blueberries but eating one or more every single day is an obsession that is not related to the real reason for food, survival – nothing more. We should look to experience flavours and delight in all our choices, because food can be one of life's greatest pleasures and casually eating the same food every single day to relentless levels moves the taste to blasé eating. Think about your own relationship to food and how it reflects a time-honoured true source of energy. What happens when you overwater a plant or feed it too many nutrients? Most of the modern obesity problem stems from a massive availability of food year-round and an individual's difficulty in controlling their will. Removing the system is not possible so the will must be managed by meaning and relationship.

## SSF Protocol

I begin with the clearest of prescriptions for all clients to make this happen. At KongDay we suggest that the first nutritional change to make is by following a SS (F) protocol. This requires minimising your intake of salts and sugars. Depending on your daily metabolic demands this also might mean adapting your fats. Now I want to etch this SS (F) formula in your mind using some stark symbolism.

The SS was the elite guard of the Nazi Reich. Those responsible for enforcing terror. If you go high on salt and sugar, you have let the SS into your body and they are on the loose. The (F), fats, are the key caveat here and we will call them The Führer, the German word for leader but usually associated with Hitler himself. A leader is important (good fats, which we need) but a bad one is worse than no leader (bad fats). Fats are extremely important and can be consumed safely and healthily to high levels (unlike sugar and salt), to aid protection of your organs, cell function, uptake of nutrients and more. And yet, so much nutritional guidance over the past few decades has painted 'fat' as a catch-all number one health enemy, when it's not. So much food labelling will focus on 'low fat', and yet sneak in high levels of the far-worse salt and sugar! We will look later at good and bad fat in more detail but do not let the SS into your house relentlessly.

# Whole ingredients

Once you have started thinking about the SS and its Führer, the next important step is to choose food which remains in its whole state and contains no other ingredients. This should be very easy to do but is near impossible in today's supermarkets. It has been estimated that over 50% of the calories consumed by the average UK consumer are from ultra-processed foods, ie ones which are produced industrially with a huge list of 'added ingredients'. That is 1 in 2 of every bite for a nation. A great way to start is to buy only items that contain three or less ingredients on the label. Forget looking at the calorie count on the label and just simplify the ingredients you are consuming to be what they are, not joined with dozens of friends.

# Ignore the headlines!

As I've already mentioned, nutrition advice is often misleading, wrong or sensationalist. Crazy headlines such as 'Eating eggs is worse than smoking' or 'vegan diets cause depression' are always based on selective data and are often the result of research by vested interests from the food industry. You will all have your own examples, and I have conducted a great deal of research myself in this area, so I hope we can cut through all this by offering you some straightforward advice.

# Research yourself

Instead of being pulled this way and that by the latest nutrition 'research', formulate your own tested conclusions. Do this aligned to the nature of scientific testing, in creating hypotheses that prove theory wrong. You want to celebrate by finding that things do not work. In this model you then uncover what is negligible but also what shows effect for you directly. Do this by carrying out your own long-term study of what foods and differing nutrition does for you. To do this you just need to eat loads of different foods and undertake different macronutrient approaches. You have every day and every experience unique to you to test. You can assess how you feel energy wise and internally after various different foods. You can see how different food and timings affects your sleep, energy levels and daily scores. Take a tomato, how does it differ when it's eaten for breakfast or in the evening? How do the methods of cooking it change the taste and effect to you? What do you need to pair this food with? Push yourself and begin to trial different ways and varying foods for long periods and then make assessments for what works best for you. A glucose monitor is one easy way to do this.

# Go Blue Zone

Geographical areas around the world act as outliers and beat the odds for the percentage of people that live to be healthy and over 100 years of age. These are termed *'blue zones'* and range from South America to Europe to Japan, so location doesn't stand out as a reason that could be the justification for aging well. What better data could you want than witnessing large communities with high numbers of people who are over 100 years of age? It doesn't really matter what is reported in studies; these people are alive and their communities are clearly documented.

The key author of the blue zone study, Dan Buettner, attributed the achievement of a long life span to two factors: nutrition and community. We will look at the importance of community later in the chapter on relationships but nutrition is focused on here. Buettner produced an excellent breakdown of the five different blue zone eating habits in his recipe book *100 Recipes to Live to 100* which I will simplify below (regardless of geographical area):

- Whole foods
- 90-100% plant-based

- Fruits, nuts, vegetables, tubers, beans, whole grains
- High fibre

This might seem extremely simple but this is the reality of these areas. Their food has not been over complicated. I have found it requires a change from expensive gadgets and western lazy food preparation to truly make the mindset shift. Choosing simple recipes that you like and for most people finding the ones which are easy to prepare becomes key. In blue zones, members of the community are happy spending hours preparing, sourcing and cooking food, not something most reading this book will want to do. And, interestingly, because of the time spent on the food preparation process, overeating is hard – they are too busy to snack! BlueZoners do not seem to eat very much. So, what approaches can we add to our routine to bring down total consumption? For many of my athletes this is done by ensuring a busy morning. Lack of time makes an early morning fast easier and can then be a simple way to bring down total calories. It also can limit insulin spiking with this approach.

Indeed, I conducted a research paper during my masters which contradicted the common athletic approach of utilising sugar and glucose to increase performance. Outside of ultra-marathons I personally questioned the real need to add fast sugars or electrolytes as a fuel source, yet many companies' products in the health space are full of such compositions (my wife calls me the sugar police). I did not believe that this was a healthy route long-term for people. If you rely for a decade of competing by snacking and fueling with high sugar products, what happens after you stop competing? It is then not easy to break the habit, so my research focused on assessing the effects lower sugar levels had on competition performance first because athletes don't care about life after competing while they are still focused on winning. My study of mixed martial artists found that after an initial dip the athletes continued to hit performance improvements regardless of the missing sugar boost. The conclusion, although conducted on a small and unique data set, was that when the competitors consumed daily sugar intake over 50g they were pushed closer toward a sympathetic nervous system reading in their heart rate variability monitoring. Sugar is not bad – it is the human ability to control the sugar or even know the hidden sugar society is secretly feeding them.

What happens when you omit or change your food choices? Perhaps your energy levels are the direct response to food timings and food choice.

Often the hardest acceptance is what is happening here. We can take truth just from an 'expert' informing us of what will occur. I remember being convinced by the spiritualist Sadhguru that drinking a daily cup of warm water with a spoon of raw honey was optimal to feed both body and brain with its essential glucose. However, it wasn't until I looked at the rest of his guidance that called for eating only once a day. His approach did not fit my lifestyle and energy demands. *Too many people want to tell you what to do based on what works for them.* I find that even a healthy morning sweet drink kicks my system off to crave more sweetness. When I just have water or black coffee I do not want sweet foods. Our desire for ever sweeter foods is evident in the modern-day breeding of fruit. Continual varieties have produced sweeter and sweeter fruits. Compare most apples now to a crab apple. I expect most reading this book cannot even eat a crab apple. That used to be a sweet food! We need to be careful about where our small actions will lead us, especially in nutrition.

## Food timing

Using the measurement of calories, we all have a rough idea of what we think we should eat per day for health. This will depend on our frame, activity level and genetics but the variance is often minimal. However, what can make a significant difference is the timing of when you consume those calories. If you consume 2000 calories a day, is it better to do that in 4 small 500 calorie servings or one massive portion? Of course, I cannot answer this for you and right now you probably can't. But in your quest to work on your nutrition you should be able to. At present, I have arrived at my optimal nutrition by eating just two meals a day. The first around lunchtime and the second around 5pm. That's it. No breakfast, no snacks. If I have an intensive muscular-training day, I add either a snack or another meal. As my work schedule changes and my environment shifts, I will tweak and test how changing this affects my HRV, sleep and energy levels. Some find greater success eating just once per day, others multiple times. Age will also likely influence your performance. But one clear advantage I have found for most people is to stop snacking.

## Stop snacking!

Do we need to snack? What exactly is the benefit of snack periods during the day? It is hard to argue for any valid answer except as being for the benefit of food product sales representatives. A snack in ancient times would have really been a meal to keep going in the quest for significant calories. It was also consumed on the move in our nomadic culture. Today, even healthy foods as snacks may be a problem in that they are messing with our hormones upon consumption and contain significant calories for such a small offering. A small bar might advertise it is only 200 calories but consider a 100g serving of cod is under 100 calories. Solely on common sense, we understand that fat cells release the sugar they hold upon our non-eating periods. Optimal weight and sugar levels in the body therefore become hard to achieve with snacking. On top of this, constant small snacking periods take time. Remove them and you might find an extra 10 minutes per day for focusing on your goal.

Until around 3 years ago, I was always snacking. I would tell myself a handful of nuts was healthy and so was beneficial. The change came from having a young child. In raising kids there is a real argument for creating routines. I was someone who knew the importance of organisation and scheduling and yet never viewed snacks as contradicting my belief. Not giving my child snacks throughout the day was met with huge resistance. I would be at parks or days out and find people offering my child snacks. We had never had a problem with our son eating. Not snacking meant he was hungry at designated mealtimes and would then eat three times per day. When snacking broke this routine, we would witness mood swings and a change in behaviour. Children's snacks (adults' too really) are nowadays always sweet because how else do you get children to eat? It still astonishes me daily to go to the school pick-up and see 90% of the children immediately consuming a sugary, non-nutritious snack. It baffles me that a host of modern problems such as mental health, obesity and concentration are rarely linked by parents to this behaviour. What use anyway is a 'treat' such as an ice cream or a pack of sweets when it's consumed every day? It's now not a treat or reward, it's the norm.

## What's your eating window?

A great book to read to further this discussion is *The Circadian Code* by Dr Satchin Panda. In his book Panda discusses the role that the circadian rhythm plays in affecting our nutrition and health. We all give our digestive system a rest by the window when we sleep yet we are unaware this time spent may not be a long enough break.

People, either in meals or snacks, often consume food for 15 or more hours daily. If you analyse your own eating window – how long is it from start to finish each day? Longer periods may be the cause for affecting your energy levels and weight loss and something which will heavily affect your circadian rhythm.

If you feel that fluctuating energy levels and/or bowel movements are affecting you I would urge you to make this one of your first changes in your nutrition approach. Earlier we discussed the importance of light for sleep, and eating is similar. In periods of longer daylight, you might have a longer eating window as when paired with sleep you might also be awake more. Having a late evening meal in summertime may not be as bad for your hormonal system as in the winter. If you live in Alaska or similar climates where periods of light can be all day during summer to almost minimal in winter, then this may be further exacerbated. Understanding your own context and environment is essential to figure out and construct an optimal nutrition strategy.

Also, you will need to consider the role foods play. Caffeine, alcohol and heavier meals require a longer time to be moved through your system. Many cultures drink a glass of alcohol at lunch as opposed to in the evening. The nutrition and composition have not changed but the timing to your system has.

Ultimately Dr Panda sets his own recommendation of limiting yourself to a 12-hour eating window, giving a guaranteed 12-hour window of rest for the digestive system. This is a great starting point for most people. Let's now look to an area which extends this concept further, something which has recently been receiving a lot of support for its potential health benefits; restricted eating and fasting.

# Restricted eating

The problem with restricting your time window of eating is immediately we face something we are no longer used to. Nowadays we seem to eat all the time and food is everywhere so refraining from this seems like a diet or unhealthy because it is restrictive. Ultimately it again is only successful with a reframing of the mind. We have become conditioned to being able to access food at every turn. People dieting often follow a caloric deficit regime, but they still eat whenever they like and so struggle due to often feeling hungry.

The first and main benefit that you should focus upon from restrictive eating is what I began this chapter writing about, in *creating the foundation to change your mindset towards food*. After you have become used to the initial hunger pangs that arise at the usual times you eat, you will find that your energy levels will increase despite not eating. Do this for long enough and your body and brain will be used to the new times of eating. Breakfast for most of my clients has been the area that had previously been an essential to function and move. After continually adhering to no breakfast the very same people later find it hard to want breakfast in the morning. We are simply forged by our habits. Additionally, you might notice that the flavours and your enjoyment of food increase due to actually being hungry when you eat rather than just auto piloting food down your throat. Take a food that you might currently consume a few times per week, let's say bananas or bacon. Ignoring the nutritional value of the food in question, the nature of regular consumption diminishes your system's ability to notice how salty, fatty or sweet the food tastes. However, as you refrain from eating that food for a few months, the return to eating it may also be accompanied by a huge salty or sweet shock. Much like the drinker who after years can consume massive amounts of alcohol without receiving the same buzz, the human body adapts to what it consumes regularly. So, without the sudden clarity and indeed reflection gained by cutting out a regular foodstuff, it is easy to see how we can develop so many unhealthy habits, especially in our food choices. With many of us being spoilt for endless food choices year-round it doesn't hurt any of us to realise our privilege and suffer like the many worldwide who face daily hunger. We can improve our nutrition health simply by being more thankful for our situation.

I remember reading a book titled *The Bible of Coffee* which uttered a barista's dismay at adding milks to coffee bean. You do not taste the flavours of that bean. Want some ketchup with your steak? What are we really tasting? All the time we are masking and distorting flavours and ingredients simply out of habit.

# Fasting

I first stumbled upon the benefits of fasting in my journey to cutting weight as a competitive fighter. While it can be extremely dangerous this is only as a result of a loss of hydration. Most people do not understand that you do not lose much weight initially by not eating. It is when you stop drinking that weight loss will accelerate dangerously. Please understand that I am not encouraging anyone to decrease fluid consumption. The images you may have seen of fighters falling out of saunas and looking extremely gaunt, unable to move for lack of energy is solely water loss. I learnt early from boxing that losing weight was okay as long as it wasn't via massive dehydration. Too many boxers had died from draining their body of the protective water that surrounds the brain and organs. You don't even need to be punched to suffer, witness those stuck in the wilderness or marathoning, dehydration is deadly.

During my method of bringing my weight down for competition (consuming fewer calories and prioritising higher protein and fat consumption over carbs) I would often ask myself why I didn't eat like this all the time. This was because I often felt like I had more energy through eating less and my skin always improved. Blood biomarkers also showed it was having positive effects improving my cholesterol and IGF (Insulin-like Growth Factor) scores, things I could monitor easily in the US at the time (note – this is less straightforward to do in other countries).

So, if I was improving my energy levels, skin tone and weight level by altering my diet, what could be achieved if I stopped eating anything for a significant period of time? In other words, fasting. The goal here is to achieve a high level of ketosis and cellular regeneration (more on this below), something which only fasting can achieve to significant levels, at least in my experience. For those of you unfamiliar with the term, ketosis is the process that happens when in your body there are not sufficient carbohydrates to burn for energy, and so instead the body burns fat and in doing so creates ketones, which it can then use for fuel.

# The 100-hour fast

Before we go into more detail about a specific fasting regime which has worked for me, let me just make one thing clear. In the context of the KongDay system of making consistent steady improvements to the 5 key areas of your life, fasting is at the extreme end of things. With my background in elite sport, fasting is discussed and practised widely. Within the general population, think of it as a 'nutritional extreme sport'. You need to build up to it, and if you decide that it's never going to be something you want to try, *this does not undermine your KongDay plan*. However, I can testify to the unique benefits that fasting can bring, so I would like to share this with you.

I have arrived at an optimal annual fasting regime to follow, which includes two periods of 100-hour fasts in a year. Do not be freaked out by this number! I have built up to this over time and I encourage starting out with far smaller regular restrictive periods that do not mean days without food. Simple 20-24hr fasts are easily and safely achieved by many people and play a solid monthly strategy to experiment upon.

For me though, I now undertake the 100-hour (4 days) fast at various points in the year. I have just concluded my second for the year before midsummer. It is essentially four days of water only. You can add in some bone broth or sodium type drinks to help with fluid retention. One of the leading experts in this field is Dr D'Agostino who recommends fasting for long periods but whilst consuming 300-500 calories of fat per day. The goal is that any fasting method should produce a high state of ketosis and cellular regeneration, and D'Agostino has found that letting people have 500 calories and under of the correct fat only brings the same benefits and makes the protocol easier to follow than consuming nothing.

I used to avoid exercise during fasting but now I find this makes ketosis harder and exercise gives me a distraction to stop the hunger. In my own experience fasting becomes very easy after **48hrs**. The real challenge after this period becomes wanting to eat again and so importance should be placed on helping your system ease back into food. The lack of stomach fluids and electrolytes that can arise can be dangerous and cause death if you do not refeed correctly. I should note that personally I do not believe this to be a concern even for 100-hour fasts. I think you would have to double the length to over 10 days to see more problems arising due to *refeeding syndrome*.

# Analysing your fast

To help produce quantitative scores and ensure you track data we need to discuss the best assessment methods during a fast. The número uno for me is to monitor ketones levels because they reflect the chemical produced when fats are broken down. This methodology is used in diabetes testing to check for dangers by showing signs of diabetic ketoacidosis (DKA) within the patient's blood or urine. *Ketosis*, on the other hand, shows the levels of *ketones* in the blood or urine and is not directly harmful. If a person was not fasting, high *ketone* levels would be a warning but during fasting it is common for *ketones* levels to rise as the chemical increases in burning stored fat.

Further to this I monitor *hematocrit* levels, which is the level by volume that red blood cells are occurring in the blood and also *haemoglobin*, which relays the level of protein molecules in the blood. Low levels of either of these would be cause for concern so they highlight a safety process that if either decreased, to stop my fast immediately regardless of how I feel. I also check body weight and bodyfat % at the beginning and the end of the 100-hour fast. You could collect more data throughout the day but I prefer to monitor these areas less as I'm not really concerned about short term changes in the markers. My data monitoring therefore looks like this when fasting:

1. Body weight
2. Body fat %

3. Hematocrit
4. Haemoglobin
5. Ketones

I choose to record 1 and 2 on my home scales despite a bone density DEXA (dual-energy X-ray absorptiometry) scan being the gold standard. Accuracy is far lower and I recommend all clients to get a DEXA scan for truly accurate body fat results. They do however incur time, effort and money which for two x-ray scans in 4 days is simply not a safe and viable option.

For factors 3-5 I receive data from a cheap and easily available ketone monitoring device to keep the process simple.

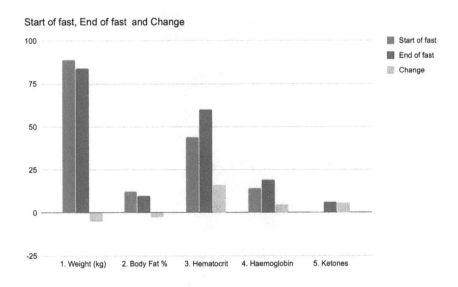

Start of fast, End of fast and Change

Here I am, looking fit (and happy!) after my 100-hour fast.

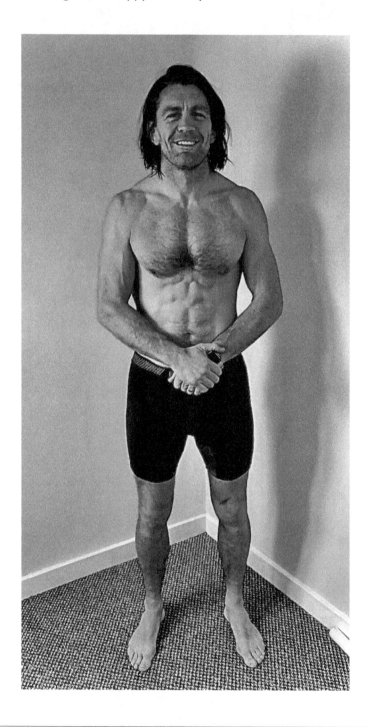

# The importance of mindset

You will have noticed that a fair bit of this nutrition chapter has already been concerned with mindset. Having the correct mindset is crucial, but all too often it is not something people consider so do not integrate into their plan. This is the only way you will change your eating goals. As soon as a mind can shift to view certain food as non-desirable then it becomes easier to avoid their consumption. You want a lifestyle where you actively choose nutritious foods because you crave their flavours not due to forced mental approach. The latter approach will never stick.

Q: Would you sign up to subscribe to the Ku Klux Klan and become a spokesperson for spreading their views? You really wish you could give up drinking soft drinks but cannot find a way? Imagine that if you drink a coke you would be announced in the national press as the new KKK lead speaker. Still not enough skin in the game to work?? Write a cheque and put it in an envelope or setup a digital transfer, to be donated should you drink the soft drink. Find strong incentives to get you off the fake food taste. Once you have time with real food you will not want to go back. Whatever you can do to change your viewpoint will make a big difference in sticking long enough to make changes. Think of something that will be a real incentive for you to make those changes and commit to it by writing it down here:

_____

_____

_____

_____

_____

_____

# Eating animal

I was raised on a small family farm and after leaving school milked cows, with fruits and vegetables being grown alongside me. Only later have I realised the privileged upbringing I had, with small family farms worldwide and ours being pushed out commercially in favour of mass scale, industrial farming. Sadly, the food system that has now been created is destroying our environment and our ecosystem. It is lost on many that there is a strong correlation between our current obesity crisis and the demise of small family farms to communities.

I'm not sure there is a more important facet to human evolution than how we eat. As a species we are now able to control other species and dominate our food supply to continuously grow and produce massive amounts of calories and waste, while leaving many still starving.

Such an extensive history of taking and destroying other species and ecosystems for this supply has led to the vegan movement, simply appealing to a greater cause of relieving animal suffering and changing land use to help tackle the problems created. These are laudable aims, but as a message unfortunately this just won't register with most people.

Instead, the main problem we now face in society is the detachment from food. We don't buy chicken with heads on, and monopolistic food brands dominate both the vegan and animal food system. We can buy foods that are laden with hidden chemicals yet be unaware of this when looking at the packaging. When you look at our current food system and see the reality of how animals are killed, people look away, yet financially support the process they look away from. As someone who has been a slaughterman and been involved in the farming process of raising and killing an animal to eat, the biggest disgust to me was always an outsider's disdain. This is where food comes from! We are happy to discuss food system effects such as plastic and pollution from our current system, but not the reality of creating most foods. Why are we turning our backs on difficult moral discussions with our children and ourselves about the food we eat? Most reading this will eat meat. When was the last time you ate lamb?

A lamb is slaughtered under the age of one year and usually far younger. That's a baby. You take children on a farm visit to discuss how cute they are yet do not turn up to witness a gunshot and hanging, followed by the skinning of the animal. If my words are already becoming too much, maybe you should continue to watch the process online. Perhaps find lambs near you and witness the full cycle of their life. If the idea of all this is too hard to bear, I do not believe you should eat meat or at least lamb. Take your child to feed the ducks and then maybe take one home and kill it together and then serve it on some rice. My words are designed to shock, but this is what we are doing and creating when we eat meat. It is the sole reason that meat is sold in large quantities because the consumer only cares for price.

If you are vegan or vegetarian, you might be unaware that the vegan system is ecologically more damaging. Remember the blue zones, where the diet is 90-95% plant based. Here, meat or fish is occasional, not 3-times-a-day consumption but it still plays a role in the system. A lot of damage to ecosystems happens when animals are removed and this is often the vegan approach. This creates an environment far from the wildlife where the nature of the food chain and a healthy ecosystem relies on the top food predators (keystone species) to balance the whole picture. I would argue that we will rapidly see development in the fake meat field via 3d printing and technological progress, but as of yet the quality is nutritionally poor.

The largest mindset shift most clients struggle to make is to build a meal that doesn't begin with (animal-based) protein at its core. Most eating windows are built around what the protein source is and the go-to for protein is animal. Most are unaware that many vegan foods you would not expect to be protein based still bring respectable protein levels to the meal. Lentils offer 8-9 grams of protein per 100g, as do oats or tofu. Rice, nuts and seeds offer around 4g per 100g serving and most vegetables will be in the 2-3g range. Building a protein-based meal is easily done without animals, indeed often the animal product on the plate might take a person's protein content over a sensible allowance for health. I do not choose to tell you whether to eat animals or not. I can support nutritional benefits for doing so and not doing so. But I would hope that in your nutrition journey you learn as much as you can about our food system and its consequences and make your food decisions from there.

# The influence of our genome

When it comes to looking at the best way to eat it is worth considering the advancements that scientific research brings. Beginning on October 1, 1990, a scientific journey began to sequence and map all the genes within Homo sapiens. Completed ahead of time in April 2003, the Human Genome Project was groundbreaking and has already helped redesign and improve treatments for multiple diseases.

For our discussion of nutrition, the genome is determining that specific individual genetics are crucial for what exactly is advantageous for you and your system. A recent project called enCode (an encyclopaedia of DNA elements) is being run by Stanford University (www.encodeproject.org) that is working on revealing answers to better structure individual nutrition. We now know that certain genomes play a role in drug metabolic rates (an example would be the tolerance to which you can handle caffeine). You will read later how HRV or glucose readings can be a simple and useful tool to advance your knowledge of personalised food responses. In the not-too-distant future it seems likely babies born will be sequenced immediately upon arrival and parents would receive a report for how to best prepare their life to their genes. Genetics can also be switched on or turned down by environment so the environment becomes the real key anyway, and one which we can already assess and reflect.

# Focus on the fundamentals

I have an overactive thyroid that means my metabolism makes it slightly easier to stay thin. Do not envy this, as it also contains health risks such as tremors, heart irregularities and losing hair, amongst others. My thyroid condition was not genetically noticeable but has likely been affected by some of my life decisions such as cutting weight and being punched in the head for well over a decade. I have spent many years getting blood results, so I have been able to spot and witness these changes as time has progressed. However, it is something I would not have noticed without monitoring. In athletic performance the term 'marginal gains' is used to describe small, minute gains that help an athlete improve. With such data I can create bespoke nutrition and help manage conditions such as thyroid or fatigue issues. The system should become a way for you to create your own nutritional science. Professor Tim Spector, who created the Zoe app to track Intermittent fasting and gut health, has recently declared that what is crucial are the times you eat rather than what you eat. Using your daily scoring of nutrition and journalling will help you piece together your own simplified hours for when to eat. You must then develop a similar focus for your nutritional needs. Looking for a quick 1% edge is not going to give you the same results as a healthy and tailored plan that is responsible for bigger percentages. A world-class athlete has long covered the fundamentals so finding a 0.5% marginal gain is worthwhile because the bigger percentages are already being met. So before you add a daily dose of blueberries you need to start to ignore the noise of marginal gains and focus on the best way to get the most likely, optimal nutrition.

# Eat more vegetables!

This slogan is spouted at children worldwide but for what reason? It is proven that vegetables and their byproducts offer protective chemicals and should form the bulk of any optimal and healthy diet. *In blue zone nutrition areas people receive over 50% of their total food from plants and a high percentage of this is vegetables.* Think about the meals you eat, is this true for you?

KongDay nutrition isn't concerned with what you can get away with, as we can witness the remarkable tolerance of the human body to tolerate poor nutrition, but rather how we can optimise and upgrade your current intake to feel better and stronger. This should be done by high-nutrient food. Consuming fresher and more nutrient-dense vegetables is also better for your microbiome. I also encourage many to spend short periods of time (consider a few days to a week) eating only vegetables and fruit. No calorie counting or restrictions placed, simply aim for an 80/20 vegetable/fruit split to avoid too much sugar. This split is not set in stone and is ultimately adaptable by your needs and desires. After doing this how do you feel and how does it change your thought of what a future nutrient-rich plate of food looks like?

# The benefits of quercetin

Quercetin is a plant pigment that has antioxidant and anti-inflammatory effects and is found primarily in fruits and vegetables. Quercetin is available as a supplement but is found highest in plants. Quercetin is potentially the reason plant-based diets are optimal for health. Plants and foods such as apples, onions, berries, along with drinks like green tea and red wine contain high amounts of the quercetin plant pigment. Looking back to the blue zones perhaps it's the high quercetin levels of the foods these areas consume that could be the hidden secret behind healthy aging. We have drummed this message into our children, but fruits, and even more so vegetables, really are the most important energy we can consume. So, make sure to make them a daily habit. Why not double your five a day to 10 (made up of mostly vegetables) and see how you feel.

# Food texture and composition

A gorilla spends most of his day chewing and there is something we can all take from this process. Choosing to eat hard foods means more time chewing (something beneficial for teeth and mouth health) and less time eating. We also fill up quicker. Maybe that handful of nuts we omitted as a snack can be a good starter at mealtimes when it is no longer a snack. Sandrine Thuret, a neuroscientist studying neurogenesis (how the adult brain produces new brain cells) lists hard foods as essential to helping the brain generate new neurons. Other notable factors that help this brain cell production process are:

- Calorie restriction of 20-30%
- Intermittent fasting
- Increasing your flavonoids (Blueberries/dark chocolate)
- A diet higher in Omega 3 fatty acids as opposed to saturated fat

Further to texture, the composition of foods has a secret. The gardeners among you might know that tomatoes take a lot of watering. The finished product is 95% water! High-water foods, like harder foods, fill you up more. There is another food higher in water content than tomatoes, but I'll let you research that yourself... This way of nutrition and eating can be termed satiety, the ability to make us feel full and keep hunger at bay.

# Fullness factor

If you are like me then you might class yourself as extremely greedy. I absolutely love food and can never remember a time in my life when I haven't wanted to eat lots of it. I often finish meals and already think about what's next to eat and scan my surroundings for something else. To help to combat this innate desire, I focus on foods with a high level of satiety or also listed towards a 'fullness factor'. A full list of these is available online and for those interested it might surprise you: nutritiondata.self.com/topics/fullness-factor. Here is a list of the top 10 foods that fill you up (on a pound for pound basis) according to science:

1. Bean sprouts
2. Watermelon
3. Grapefruit
4. Carrots

5. Oranges
6. Boiled fish
7. Chicken breast
8. Apples
9. Sirloin steak
10. Oatmeal

Potato, popcorn (although this doesn't seem to work for me at the cinema) and bananas are also close to making the top 10.

A pattern should be beginning to become clear. Eating fibre and water-based foods is often a great decision for your health. Some may include high carbohydrates or fat, to which you simply need to consider how often you consume them and your activity/lifestyle. Often non-animal protein helps people's health because it contains significantly fewer calories but the sourcing of this without a mix of processed ingredients is far harder. In my experience *the macronutrient content of food is not as important as you think — simply eat nutrient dense foods that feed your inner microbes and hunger levels.*

# The importance of your microbiome

I have recently become fascinated with nature and the complex web of interactions you can witness anywhere in the ecosystem. From tending my garden, I have learnt the ultimate power comes from what I cannot see. The world within the soil is full of billions of organisms in just one handful. Similarly, there is emerging science making it clear that the bacteria and microbes within the human gut might be the key ingredient for disease, mood, energy levels and health.

I believe the simplest way to create nutrient diverse food is to grow your own vegetables in your own healthy soil. At present I do this in the preceding year's woodchip. Simply get some hardwood diverse woodchip and spread them in the garden. A cardboard layer placed over the grass helps prevent weeds and grass growing through the bed. After 6-9 months the woodchip will become spectacular soil which you can plant in and have little need to water or weed. The woodchip mulch will ensure the crop is rigorous for all seasons and you can then pick the vegetables and immediately ferment, using simple recipes. We need a gut system that is resilient to the modern-day bombardment of pollution and toxins, and I have yet to find any other method that comes close to healing many of the autoimmune problems, other than simply fasting, which of course we can't do forever.

*Most of the fruit and vegetables I eat from my garden will be covered with insect holes and marks.* In parts of Japan consumers will pay almost double for produce containing such blemishes because the food signifies health in that the insects want to eat the food! Contrast this with our food system where all these foods do not even make it into the supermarket. I will leave this process here, but you can see on my Instagram (@tomkongwatson) and in various sources online how to ferment and extend the shelf life and vitamin content of vegetables regardless of how they look.

# The early years are crucial

Worryingly, evidence suggests that alongside our genetics the formative early years of life affects much of our later health, regardless of how we act now. Henna-Maria Uusitupa paints a gloomy picture in her Ted talk, *How the gut microbes you're born with affect your lifelong health*. In this, she essentially states that your birth is the pivotal determinant to your later microbiome health. This sadly returns us back to the theme of things we cannot control. You had no say on whether you were breastfed or how you were raised as a child. Obesity is higher in young children who were heavily treated with antibiotics in early life. Cardiovascular diseases are statistically higher in babies born by caesarian section. We cannot control any of these early life actions, but we can influence our microbiome colonisation and alter its hosts to be beneficial for the body, starting today.

At present you likely have no idea on the species residing in your gut. The starting point then is to get some data on the current microbes within the gut and address actions for positive change. The normal process is to go out and buy probiotic and/or prebiotic supplements which currently offer little evidence to justify their need. For me a constant challenge is irritable and dry skin due I believe, to being prescribed Roaccutane as a teenager for severe acne. Add in the continual extreme exercise in my 20s for my career and the aggravation was daily. For others it might be IBS (irritable bowel syndrome), now one of the most common disorders worldwide with as many as 45% globally suffering from the condition. Instead of simply ordering random supplements and hoping for the best, begin by ordering a microbiome test.

*Do it now! [and tick the box here when you have done so!]*

This field is advancing rapidly, and new companies are appearing all the time. Currently a test will cost around £110, and results can be presented like those below from my first microbiome test I performed with Atlas Biomed many years ago.

## Microbiome case study

Below are reproduced images and text from the microbiome test I undertook.

Your microbiome is organised into one of three types that have been established by analysing thousands of samples from around the world. Large-scale metagenomic studies have identified "enterotypes": stable combinations of bacteria co-existing in communities. Each person's microbiome falls into one of these three groups, which correspond with different styles of nutrition. Your microbiome type can change should you significantly modify your diet or be subjected to external factors.

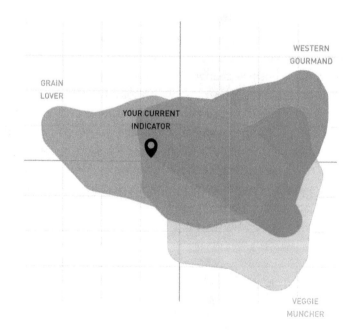

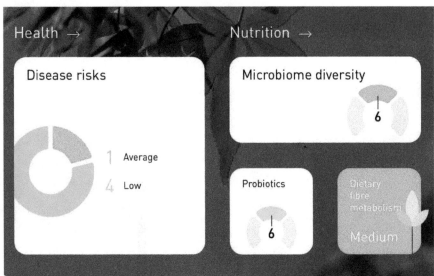

Health →

Nutrition →

## Disease risks

1 Average

4 Low

## Microbiome diversity

6

### Probiotics

6

### Dietary fibre metabolism

Medium

## Insights →

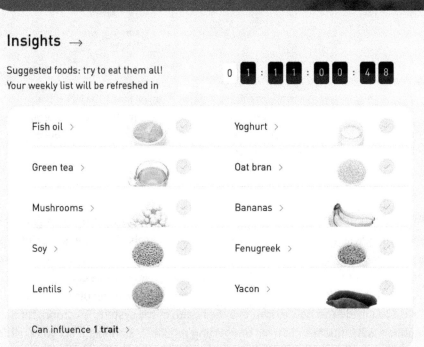

Suggested foods: try to eat them all!
Your weekly list will be refreshed in

0 1 : 1 1 : 0 0 : 4 8

| Fish oil > | | | Yoghurt > | | |
| Green tea > | | | Oat bran > | | |
| Mushrooms > | | | Bananas > | | |
| Soy > | | | Fenugreek > | | |
| Lentils > | | | Yacon > | | |

Can influence **1 trait** >

## Shannon Index

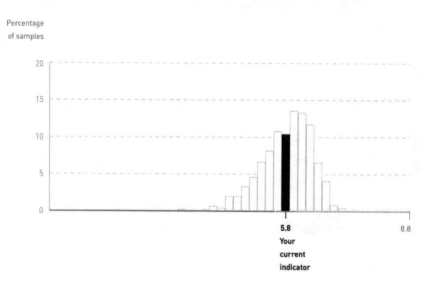

Microbiome diversity is calculated using the Shannon index. The higher the index value, the more types of bacteria in your colon and the better it is for your health and wellbeing. You can also see how your diversity compares to other Atlas users in the Shannon graph.

This test immediately made me realise that I needed to eat more vegetables and perhaps have less grain in my diet. You will likely also have areas to celebrate and areas to improve upon receiving results. Upon repeating the test 6 months later my Shannon Index score had risen to 7.1 with a few simple changes. I do not place 100% validity to the test but when combined with regular blood work I have a rough idea on how to improve the health of my system. Environment and situation will influence changes but getting regular 2-3 annual tests will enable you to formulate a baseline of your gut health. You should then be able to reveal the ways in which various food types benefit or adversely affect you.

Genetically my data coincided with information my mother had received that she was registering as pre-diabetic (despite being a healthy body weight for her age, running regularly and cooking most of her meals). I decided that pushing my diet further away from a western gourmand grouping (one of animal fats, protein and refined sugar) towards a veggie muncher was a good strategy. After I received my initial microbiome results, I looked back at my journalling and saw I was still eating the occasional pastry, desserts and meat during this time. Coupling this with my neurological concern of likely future cognitive decline I decided I was not doing enough. I chose to increase fibre to well over 50g per day. I had been consuming what I thought was a lot of fibre compared to others but at best I was averaging 20-25g per day. The Blue Zones nutrition again became a simple path to see what foods I could increase my fibre content. Let's review the top ten foods from each blue zone:

(I have highlighted in bold the foods that we could consider high in sugar)

SARDINIA:
1. Barley
2. Fava beans
3. Kohlrabi
4. Fennel
5. Potatoes
6. Sourdough bread
7. Tomatoes
8. Rosemary
9. Olive oil
10. **Cannonau wine**

OKINAWA:
1. Imo
2. Dashi broth
3. Green onions
4. Miso
5. Sesame oil
6. Seaweed
7. Tofu
8. Turmeric
9. Mushrooms
10. Goya

## NICOYA:

1. Sweet peppers
2. Ground corn
3. Coriander
4. Coconut
5. Chilero sauce
6. Papaya
7. Yuca
8. Squash
9. Culantro
10. Black beans

## IKARIA:

1. Beans
2. Wild greens
3. Lemons
4. Fennel
5. Olive oil
6. Potatoes
7. Sage
8. Rosemary
9. **Honey**
10. Oregano

## LOMA LINDA:

1. **Soy milk**
2. Corn flakes
3. Brewers' yeast
4. **Weetabix**
5. Nuts
6. Avocados
7. Beans
8. Spinach
9. Vegemite
10. Oatmeal

1. _____

2. _____

3. _____

4. _____

5. _____

6. _____

7. _____

8. _____

9. _____

10. _____

# It's not your fault!

I want to now conclude this chapter on nutrition by repeating, as I do to clients: *give yourself a break, it is not your fault*. We blame ourselves because we are the ones who choose what we put in our mouths but forget that evolutionary factors and life have heavily influenced this behaviour. We crave sugar because this is a guaranteed method to help us store more fat. The ancestral need for hibernation in cold weather in a completely different landscape to how we live now still triggers why we desire fat stores but of course we no longer live with the same requirements. Understand that genetic or evolutionary cravings will always exist but recognise that consistent, daily habits will reduce such cravings.

Eating sweet foods can be advocated in an approach championed by Michael Pollen. Pollen wrote *The Omnivore's Dilemma* and argues that you can pretty much eat whatever you want as long as you source ingredients and make all the food yourself. He references living on apple pie, all day, every day, to make his point. You just need to source and make all parts of the pie yourself.

I hope I have presented a case here for you to learn and understand the food system to help your nutrition. I will further add that preparing your food is the next stage. I will not however write here about cookery masterclasses or recommend top chefs you can learn from. I will simply advise that an easy place to start cooking is to use recipe books that only have 4 items maximum per recipe. The flavours and meal may not be as mesmerising, but they are far easier to cook when starting out. Remember, creating a habit needs an easy start and cooking is no different. Cooking is actually very easy, enjoyable, and largely a social event worldwide. I have found that using a cheap slow cooker is ideal for most beginners. Chop (or use a mechanical chopping device) and throw everything in and hours later you have a meal with no effort.

I will never forget taking a private cooking course in Orange County, California with my wife (girlfriend at that time), run by Michelin-star chef Conrad Gallagher. Gallagher earned two Michelin stars as owner of Peacock Alley in Dublin between 1998 and 2002. He later moved to open restaurants in Las Vegas and California, cooking for US presidents. I learnt a great deal about the importance of sourcing fresher ingredients and the simplicity of using spices for flavouring but I also witnessed the other side of restaurant food. His unique secret to the best mashed potato is "putting as much cream in as potato". I loved to frequent Michelin star food but viewed the food there as healthy. Despite being fresh and nutrient dense, many of the world's best restaurants are serving up rich, heavily salted, fatty and sugary courses. I am not against this food as an occasional treat but in taking methods back for my own cooking practice, not so much. Perhaps this is why chefs also seem to carry quite a few extra pounds... We return back to the SS (F) principle. If your taste buds are already deeply immersed in this way of eating, start by lowering salt, sugar and fat minimally. A complete cut off probably won't work. If your coffee takes 3 sugars slowly progress down to 1. Then maybe use a stevia or alternative until you drink coffee with no sweeteners. But have a plan and a timeline. Do not randomly decide when you will reach the desired levels, or you never will.

*"Happiness is a good bank account, a good cook and a good digestion."*

Jean-Jacques Rousseau

# Key Implementations:
## Nutrition

> Consider the food you are eating by how it is produced and made.

> Eat whole foods.

> Make food as much a part of community as opposed to eating just for fuel.

> Eat more vegetables. Change your culture so breakfast is not only cereals or eggs/bread/cheese.

> Grow more food. You don't need a big garden. Work with any space you have.

> If you eat meat, understand the whole process of raising animals. Know the source and make your decisions.

> If eating fish, consider the sustainability guide when buying. Eating fish every day is not healthy or sustainable, especially with the current pollution of our oceans and planet.

> Conclude by adhering to SS (F) principles. Lowering your salt and sugar intake is a must. Fat is lifestyle dependent.

# My Nutrition Score charts for 2020

Nutrition - Visual Shades

| | JAN | FEB | MAR | APR | MAY | JUN | JUL | AUG | SEP | OCT | NOV | DEC |
|---|---|---|---|---|---|---|---|---|---|---|---|---|
| 1 | 3 | 3 | 3 | 3 | 4 | 3 | 3 | 2 | 4 | 3 | 4 | 3 |
| 2 | 4 | 3 | 1 | 3 | 4 | 1 | 3 | 2 | 4 | 3 | 3 | 3 |
| 3 | 4 | 3 | 3 | 3 | 5 | 3 | 4 | 3 | 3 | 4 | 2 | 3 |
| 4 | 4 | 3 | 3 | 3 | 3 | 4 | 3 | 4 | 2 | 3 | 3 | 2 |
| 5 | 3 | 3 | 2 | 3 | 2 | 4 | 4 | 2 | 3 | 4 | 2 | 4 |
| 6 | 3 | 3 | 3 | 2 | 2 | 4 | 4 | 2 | 3 | 2 | 2 | 4 |
| 7 | 3 | 4 | 3 | 4 | 2 | 3 | 4 | 2 | 3 | 3 | 4 | 4 |
| 8 | 2 | 3 | 1 | 2 | 3 | 5 | 3 | 2 | 3 | 3 | 3 | 4 |
| 9 | 4 | 1 | 4 | 3 | 2 | 3 | 3 | 5 | 3 | 2 | 4 | 5 |
| 10 | 5 | 2 | 4 | 4 | 3 | 4 | 4 | 5 | 4 | 1 | 4 | 4 |
| 11 | 4 | 3 | 3 | 5 | 2 | 3 | 3 | 3 | 1 | 3 | 4 | 4 |
| 12 | 3 | 2 | 3 | 4 | 3 | 3 | 4 | 4 | 4 | 3 | 3 | 4 |
| 13 | 3 | 4 | 3 | 4 | 2 | 3 | 4 | 3 | 4 | 2 | 4 | 4 |
| 14 | 3 | 1 | 3 | 4 | 3 | 3 | 2 | 3 | 4 | 4 | 4 | 4 |
| 15 | 3 | 2 | 4 | 4 | 2 | 4 | 3 | 4 | 4 | 4 | 3 | 3 |
| 16 | 4 | 3 | 2 | 5 | 2 | 4 | 4 | 3 | 4 | 2 | 4 | 3 |
| 17 | 2 | 3 | 3 | 4 | 3 | 4 | 4 | 4 | 4 | 2 | 4 | 3 |
| 18 | 3 | 3 | 4 | 4 | 4 | 4 | 4 | 4 | 3 | 4 | 4 | 1 |
| 19 | 3 | 4 | 3 | 4 | 2 | 4 | 4 | 4 | 4 | 3 | 3 | 4 |
| 20 | 2 | 3 | 3 | 3 | 3 | 3 | 4 | 2 | 4 | 4 | 3 | 3 |
| 21 | 2 | 2 | 3 | 3 | 3 | 4 | 5 | 3 | 2 | 3 | 3 | 3 |
| 22 | 4 | 1 | 2 | 2 | 4 | 4 | 4 | 3 | 3 | 3 | 4 | 3 |
| 23 | 4 | 1 | 3 | 3 | 4 | 3 | 2 | 1 | 4 | 3 | 4 | 1 |
| 24 | 4 | 1 | 3 | 2 | 4 | 4 | 3 | 3 | 4 | 3 | 5 | 1 |
| 25 | 3 | 3 | 3 | 3 | 5 | 3 | 1 | 3 | 2 | 3 | 5 | 3 |
| 26 | 3 | 2 | 2 | 3 | 1 | 2 | 1 | 4 | 4 | 3 | 4 | 3 |
| 27 | 3 | 3 | 2 | 3 | 3 | 3 | 4 | 3 | 4 | 3 | 4 | 4 |
| 28 | 3 | 1 | 2 | 3 | 4 | 2 | 3 | 3 | 4 | 3 | 2 | 3 |
| 29 | 2 | 3 | 3 | 4 | 2 | 2 | 4 | 3 | 4 | 3 | 3 | 3 |
| 30 | 1 | | 2 | 4 | 5 | 2 | 4 | 3 | 3 | 3 | 3 | 3 |
| 31 | 4 | | 4 | | 4 | | 2 | 4 | | 3 | | 2 |

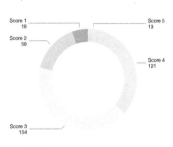

Nutrition - Year Score Count

Score 1
19

Score 2
59

Score 3
154

Score 4
121

Score 5
13

Nutrition Score Counts

| | January | February | March | April | May | June | July | August | September | October | November | December | Total |
|---|---|---|---|---|---|---|---|---|---|---|---|---|---|
| Score 5 | 1 | 0 | 0 | 2 | 3 | 1 | 1 | 2 | 0 | 0 | 2 | 1 | 13 |
| Score 4 | 10 | 3 | 5 | 11 | 8 | 12 | 16 | 8 | 17 | 6 | 14 | 11 | 121 |
| Score 3 | 14 | 15 | 17 | 13 | 9 | 12 | 9 | 13 | 9 | 19 | 10 | 14 | 154 |
| Score 2 | 5 | 5 | 7 | 4 | 10 | 4 | 3 | 7 | 3 | 5 | 4 | 2 | 59 |
| Score 1 | 1 | 6 | 2 | 0 | 1 | 1 | 2 | 1 | 1 | 1 | 0 | 3 | 19 |

KONGDAY: Quantifying your life to success

# 4: PHYSICALITY

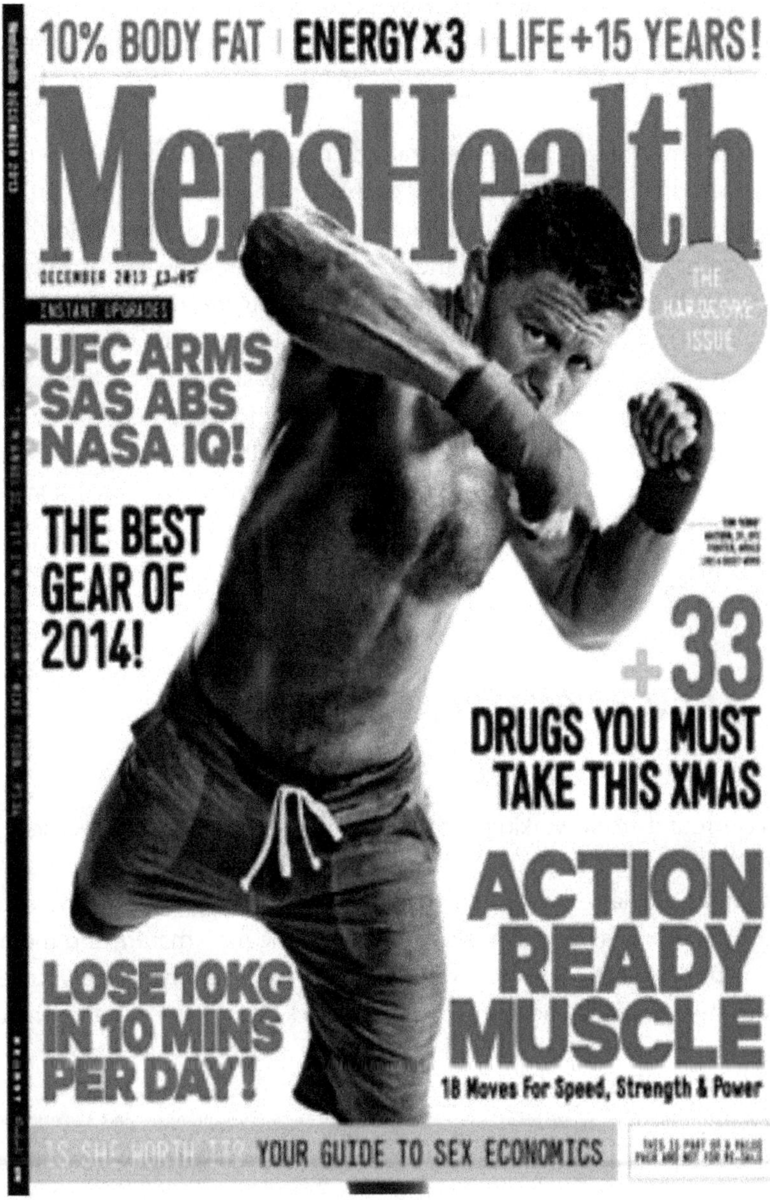
10% BODY FAT
ENERGY x3
LIFE +15 YEARS!
Men'sHealth
INSTANT UPGRADES
UFC ARMS
SAS ABS
NASA IQ!
THE BEST GEAR OF 2014!
+33 DRUGS YOU MUST TAKE THIS XMAS
ACTION READY MUSCLE
18 Moves For Speed, Strength & Power
LOSE 10KG IN 10 MINS PER DAY!
YOUR GUIDE TO SEX ECONOMICS

AS A FORMER *Men's Health* cover model, you would hope I would know something about physically working out and muscle development. My simplest takeaway message from this Physicality chapter may surprise you – *most workouts are not healthy*. This may seem hugely contradictory but stick with me. Movement and mobility are healthy for the body, both in the short and the long term, yet I have found that most physical exertion these days seems to be motivated by an aesthetic goal and an obsession with performance, rather than for improving health. What looks great on Instagram may not look great inside.

Consider that athletic bodies generally do not age well. They have been pushed beyond comfort to achieve faster and better performances but little regard has gone to long-term health. While nutrition has helped people look and stay younger at a later age, a lot of the current physicality guidance is only suitable for those between 20-45 years of age. And if you are currently within that age range you still presumably want to be as mobile as you are now, for as long as you can. Therefore, much of your physical focus should be on the importance of joint health and the structure of your muscles for consistent movement. For sure, we need to raise our heart rates and physically strain our muscles daily but take care as to the intensity and regularity of your methods if you are striving for blue zone old age.

# Regular exercise and movement

I have found from working with clients that exercise and movement is the area most immediately seek to create a healthier future. This is for good reason as regular exercise and movement are the biggest prevention aids to all-cause mortality and ill health. Again, it's time for a mantra and the one we use is **Dactive** (active daily). Every single day you need to remind yourself that movement must be performed to hold back death. The Dactive mindset is essential. What have you done today?

# Start to exercise

The problem most face is where to start. Often it is to a local gym full of static machines. To most this gym world is simply boring but if you are someone who does not find this to be true, then you have a serious advantage over others. I have spent pretty much my entire life moving through professional sport, in football and martial arts, and I have concluded that the interaction of the experience and people is the best part of physical movement.

So, finding a sport at a recreational level is normally a more successful method for beginning your physical exercise journey. I am not interested in moving beyond recreation because this system is not concerned with anything more than that. Elite performance has its own separate path, but elite performers or competitive athletes can still use this system in their life to ensure performance is coupled with a life wellness approach.

Looking back, this disconnect between the two is troubling. Look at the image of front cover fitness models. Take mine above – these individuals are snapshot posters but the imagery is not actually conveying their state of health. We cannot see their blood markers, cellular age, range of movement or inflammation levels. I have many pictures from past days where I would be chiseled like a roman statue due to spending 6-8hrs daily working out, but holistically and cellularly I was less healthy than I am now, 10 years older.

Most athletes eat a certain way that is only concerned with reaching a competition goal. It might mean over 10,000 calories daily for a swimmer or minimal consumption for a weight restricted athlete. The cover pictures themselves are edited in lighting and effect to make the image fake. This look, which now sees many becoming depressed as they hopelessly pursue it, has found its way to the public in filters that generate a brushed image. For athletes, health is not the leading goal. The body becomes merely a tool to hit the fastest times, strongest lifts or achieve a defined physical challenge – operating like the equivalent of a Formula 1 car, in constant need of replacement parts and upgrading. Soon it will be phased out for a newer model, destined for the scrap heap.

CrossFit has gained massive popularity for arguably bringing the positivity associated with athletic prowess to people who before might have been considered as a non-athlete. The brand uses its mantras to promote the healthiest buzz words of squat, lunge, lift, pull etc. but the problem is in sustainability. I have a client that was forced to undergo a complete hip reconstruction in their 40s due to unhealthy movement. The human body is incredibly robust but I'm not sure it is designed to perform any movement so repetitively other than walking (occasional running as an addition). Even then, in evolutionary terms, would ultra-marathons have been performed weekly? Food foraging and nomadic behaviour was clearly walking dominant. Continuous running needs a lot of fuelling and is not worth the total calories burned.

# Stop running!

As you can tell I have reservations too with the form of exercise probably most commonly taken up as a re-entry into the world of fitness – running. By the time most of us begin to embrace it as an exercise tool we are fraught with mobility and weight issues. You can witness athletes from countries such as Kenya, which never left such an early ancestral movement pattern, seemingly running with ease at the highest level. But for the rest of us, do you want a physical training program that is in complete contradiction to the longevity protocols that have seen blue zone centurions living well into their hundreds? You may start a running program at a later age but it is likely you will soon enough witness the joints struggling to continue this exercise pattern.

# Create a balanced program of movement

So how do those centurions live out a healthy movement lifestyle for almost 100 years? By raising their heart rate consistently and moving with freedom. Take the example of picking and working in a field. The heart rate is raised, and it is hard work, but you are unlikely to need surgery or struggle to perform these tasks as you age. So, long-term healthy exercise then I feel needs to be clearly defined as simple! The old-school outdoor type job that involves some deviation from purely linear movement is a movement towards this. If you can avoid continuous repetitive action you allow your body the ability to recover and stay mobile. Once you understand this, it is up to you how you create your physicality program. I still put my body through extreme stress by wrestling and training martial arts, but I know this is not physically optimal so limit the regularity of it. For scoring my physicality scores I need to make sure mobility weighs heavier than simply pushing my body. I also accept that my past will limit the long-term health of my joints anyhow. I encourage you all to stop looking or listening to others for the physicality secret to get in super shape. Sitting, even for fractional amounts such as an hour a day, can spell doom for the human body so let's answer some questions to get you moving.

Q: Each day, on average, how many hours do you spend sitting?

_____

How mobile are you compared to a toddler?

_____

What would be dream physicality to you?

_____

_____

The above answers should begin to help you create your own physicality program. It might not be completely focused on either the short or long-term but it's a solid starting point. You will be aware of the physical consequences of your movement actions.

# The scourge of sitting

If sitting is the new smoking, we must stop or at least mitigate the real dangers. Implement whatever you can to bring your sitting to as little as possible. Standing desks and movement timers (getting up to move every 10 minutes for example) are ways to help. Alongside this I encourage you all to begin deep squatting daily and build the length of time you stay in this position. You will need to find ways to increase your ankle and knee mobility but there is a plethora of material to help you to do so easily.

The two staples I ask all clients to work towards is 30 minutes minimum per day in deep squat and 10 mins hanging from a bar. Fear not, this is not in one hit (but could be attempted). Dropping onto a squat for a few mins regularly makes 30 minutes achievable. The same can be said for hanging. The challenge with hanging is that you will have to implement areas and devices that allow you to easily hang during your lifestyle. Those that cannot hang without assistance can do so with assistance. Progression is necessary for every person and limitations are never an excuse because you should be comparing yourself only to yourself. Poles, bars or even trees are found in many places and a branch can suffice. We evolved from a previous lifestyle of hanging and swinging, and your shoulder health and back pain will thank you for building this into your life. The challenge is always to figure out how to start small and easy. Progressing steadily towards something is always the focus rather than starting too hard and getting injured or despondent.

# The significance of telomeres

One of the most important components in achieving a healthy mind and body is that of training telomeres. Telomeres form the ends of our chromosomes, and the simplest description is that they offer a shoelace-like protective plastic capping to our bodies. Without protection, laces wear down and fray. Telomeres then can be said to mimic this role but for our cells and DNA. Telomeres are responsible for making you look like your grandfather as without telomeres genes would be lost and not passed on at all.

Physical activity is the only way you can currently influence your telomere length, so finding a way to enjoying consistent daily exercise is better than finding a few days per week over the long term. Currently, you probably build your day around work and what you have to do, but could you build your day around physicality? The answer is that yes, you can, and a great way to start is to create a planner that starts with a commitment each day to incorporate some exercise and movement. You probably already know your working schedule so where does that leave your physicality programming?

Monday: _____

Tuesday: _____

Wednesday: _____

Thursday: _____

Friday: _____

Saturday: _____

Sunday: _____

I hope you kept it simple. Forget about performing amazing athletic feats and trying to copy the 1%. Create a consistent movement program that starts small and scales up over time. Walking with additional exercise periods of resistance or HIIT (high intensity interval training) is a great way to start, regardless of your individual ability.

In my system I have worked with many successful businesspeople who tend to quickly get into a workout routine that in intensity can easily match any world-class athlete but this rigorous hour per day of physical scheduling ignores the fact that the rest of the day is spent sitting down, on the phone and barely moving from the office.

Instead, try to reframe your life's movement to then assess how that makes your body and mind feel.

# Technology overload

Wearable devices, in my opinion, have helped many people significantly up their physical performance. The daily goal of 10,000 steps is a well-known modern prescription that wearable devices are fantastic at tracking and help people move more. But technology has its problems. A friend of mine, Andy Galpin, is a tenured professor at the Center for Sport Performance at CSU Fullerton and is one of the world-leading experts in Human Bioenergetics (the transfer of energy in cells/tissues/organisms) and muscle physiology. In Dr Galpin's book *Unplugged* he concludes that utilising technology and scientific understanding to progress performance, while beneficial does have limitations; in fact his book clearly states that most people should disconnect. Galpin informs that technology at present is unable to replace the value of coach expertise and resilience training. Consider the step analysis we just described. You could walk 10,000 steps daily but in two completely different ways. Waking up to perform a run that hits 10,000 steps and then sitting for the rest of the day is not the same for your health as moving 600+ steps every hour for your health (625 steps per hour on a 16-hour schedule because we need to sleep). Most devices have adapted and use reminders to move every hour, but our movement quality is not coached.

The key way a coach can help in physicality is by increasing the level at which your mind pushes through targets. As a personal trainer I was highly sought after in my local area because I did not take the now standard personal trainer route. Most current personal trainers are greatly concerned with being sued and will keep clients on a path of safety first. For me I was more concerned about helping clients develop their mind when working out and, contradictory to my earlier advice, this often comes from pushing past what the mind thinks it is capable of. We all have the voice that tells us no more, yet with time and experience this voice appears later and later.

I am a big fan of David Goggins, and his simple approach he defined as the 40% rule. When you believe you're done you're really only 40% done. If this figure was higher, say 70 or 80%, the mind would still be ready to quit as it's almost the end. Setting a 40% assessment makes people stop thinking about finishing because they haven't even got halfway. If we look at our species, we can see in its history the amazing feats of endurance we have achieved starting from the migration of humans worldwide to current feats such as Nirmal Purja climbing 14 eight thousand metre peaks in just over six months. When faced with death or disaster it is almost incomprehensible how a small person can lift the weight of a car. The mind does not have an exit in these scenarios and there is only one result. I have a client who has been training to complete a marathon and is preparing using the smart and typical running scheduling. This training is beneficial and will see him comfortably complete the marathon but is it different to a mindset that might set pre-challenges such as running double the distance, eg 50 miles? Yes, the running coaches and people worldwide will say that is a stupid plan, but could you run 50 miles to save your family's life? What are we really training for? Mindset or tasks?

Return again to the 10,000 step-count we discussed earlier. Is it that difficult? Using an average modern height gives us a stride length of between 2.1 and 2.5 feet therefore 2000-2500 strides equate to roughly a mile walk. If we took 625 steps (using the top 2500 stride marker above) a quarter of a mile would have been walked. At a slow speed this can be achieved by walking for 5 minutes. So, if you walk for 5 minutes every hour you would hit 10,000 steps comfortably in a day. For the able-bodied person that wants to lose weight and move more it's just not an option to state you can't move 10,000 steps consistently each day.

As you move through this logic and system you will quickly scale up your targets because you will find the current base guidance of exercise far too easy. In my work with the police, both myself and much of the police are appalled at the annual physical tests officers need to pass. The powers that be have consistently made the assessments easier because they cannot be left in a situation where too many officers fail a physical assessment. Sadly, this means that the current assessment doesn't equal any real-world worth. It is a check box exercise that means most police officers can be in a dire physical health state and still pass a physical assessment. Worryingly the work of these officers often means that their life is in real danger from this softening of the assessment. Of course, none of these figures can be applied to a person with a disability or physical challenges but these people do not want to be defined by limitations. I can assure you that this grouping does not have a mental limitation and society is the group that needs adaptation. Use the individuality principle and figure out your own goals and physicality program that will put you in your best health. Just don't forget to push yourself.

# Diminishing returns

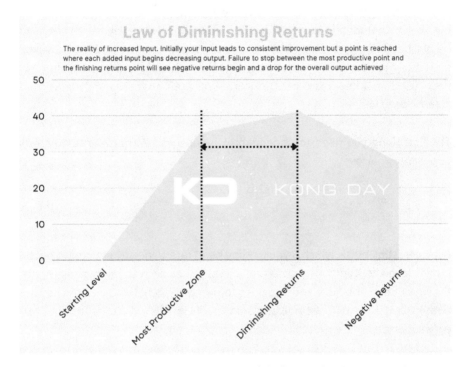

I have included the business concept of diminishing returns, as this perfectly describes physicality programming. Most people will never come close to negative returns because the human body is the ultimate machine but you should ensure that you do not over train and enter a negative return. More time will have been spent with worse results, what is the point in that? Simply the most productive zone can be hit from the starting area by a 'little and often' program. Here improvements will continue to exist and you are receiving the most bang for input buck. To ensure the training response is correct we need to understand heart rate variability and the physiology nature of the immune system.

# Reduce your resting heart rate

Understanding your heart rate is an essential tool for understanding your optimal health. The nutrients, blood and oxygen we need to stay alive are all supplied by our heart. Despite a long history of understanding pulse and the pumping nature of the heart it is only recently that the heart rate and its variability has been used as a key instrument in increasing both athletic performance and general daily health.

The first thing you need to understand is your own heart rate at rest and its upper maximal level.

## What is your pulse?

A lower resting pulse, which is your resting heart rate, generally equates to better fitness levels (except when occurring due to issues such as bradycardia where the heart beats too slow and struggles to pump oxygenated blood around the body). Many athletes in fact fall into bradycardia ranges but do not suffer health consequences.

Now take your current resting heart rate and minus 5 if it's over 60 bpm. If it is lower consider a smaller decrease.

This is now your goal – give yourself 3 months to achieve this.

Focusing on achieving a lower resting heart rate is a clear and sustainable goal. Once you reach this level and can operate continually at the new resting rate, work on steadily decreasing your resting heart rate, regardless of age.

# Tracking Heart Rate Variability (HRV)

Peak athletes often focus on their upper heart rate level, pushing this to the maximum they can. However, tracking this accurately is difficult and not as relevant to the average person as looking at HRV, so instead I want you to focus on this.

*The nervous system can be broken down into two areas, the sympathetic and the parasympathetic nervous system.*

Our heart rate reflects what our nervous system is doing. Stress, diet and exercise all play a part in affecting your variability. The sympathetic nervous system is concerned with the 'fight or flight' mode and our body's response to that stress. The opposing parasympathetic nervous system therefore restricts the body from overworking and restores the body to a calm and composed state. If you picture a set of balancing scales, I view HRV as a way of waking and using your HRV reading to decide your level of physicality and stress for the day to keep the scales even. Sometimes it needs an increase and sometimes it needs some weight removed, a pull back if you will. Generally, almost all the clients I have worked with will, after a consistent program has been established, find 1-2 days per week that they need to be rested and scaling back. Sometimes this might be 7 days of hard push followed by 2 days of rest. Many go with a fixed 1 day per week of complete rest but it should not be fixed. Life will shift the output you can create and you need to use HRV to plan attack and defence accordingly, not just deciding Sundays are your rest day every week. Most of you will not currently use HRV data but it is the simplest and best approach you can integrate for physical and balance in your life management. HRV data will reflect your life. Just because you didn't not work out yesterday your physicality may need further rest. HRV will relay the following variable inputs on your system:

- Food
- Stress
- Sleep

Once you track your HRV the three areas above will be naturally incorporated into your daily readiness score. It is easy to track your HRV and analyse your daily heart rate levels. Wearable watches or rings can do this with high accuracy and Apple even integrated their own HRV system into their watches way back in 2018.

The optimal time and way to record an accurate HRV score is upon waking, daily, for a 2-minute period. This 2-minute reading is done at the same time, position and environment every single day, thus ensuring any changes are non-environmental and purely from your internal system. If your tracking device does not produce a readiness score, then I encourage you to use a simple and free app called HRV Elite. This system https://elitehrv.com/ designed by Jason Moore, includes further options to take online courses to learn about HRV and the science behind the application. This is a great way to go beyond what is written here in understanding the HRV system.

# Case study: HRV monitoring

I have a client who is a site manager for a large European construction company. Upon tracking his HRV he became concerned with his readiness readings. Due to stress at work, he would find himself in an almost constant state of sympathetic shock. Using his data enabled us to work together to find methods that would bring his HRV up and calm his immune system. Commuting to work was a 30-minute journey and the client found using breathing exercises both on the way to work and returning became a way he could control his HRV score and calm his immune system.

He also observed that drinking alcohol (albeit only one drink a day) was adding to his sympathetic shock because of the time it was consumed. Once we could get his HRV score back on track he was able to integrate alcohol and physical exercise again and just keep an eye on his immune response to stress. Without having this data, I believe he would have found himself suffering a mental breakdown and time off work due to chronic stress.

*If we had not stopped his physical workouts and dealt with the problem, he would have continued to compound inflammation and stress. Physicality is not always the answer.*

# Focus on your own data

I hope this message will encourage you to forget listening to others about how to live and programme your day. Get your *own* data about your life and start working on your HRV and what influences it. We need to know when our system is stressed and then watch and work on rebuilding it before stressing it further. Most people say that some days they feel good, but the reality is they might not actually be good and need to undertake some stress intervention. On days I may not feel great I might wake up and receive a top 10 HRV score. Despite not feeling good I have numerical data to push myself hard physically (or mentally) in a challenge and recover faster. On the opposing viewpoint I may wake up feeling ready to attack the day but my HRV notification pulls me back. Time to scale down workouts and plans because the system is not compliant.

French-Cuban American literary powerhouse Anáis Nin stated: "Good things happen to those who hustle". Perhaps this should be rewritten as "great things come to those who hustle when their HRV says they can." We should not ever stop striving and pushing for achievements. Achievements have driven science, sport and society to unimaginable levels, but just make sure you integrate a system that informs you when to go and when to hold fire. That's all we can do to manage and live a healthy and positive life. To conclude physicality I will leave you with the following quote:

*"Those who think they have not time for bodily exercise will sooner or later have to find time for illness."*

Edward Stanley

## Case study: my own exercise journey

I will repeat again that exercise needs to be based around individual prescription. This is a simple fact that is all too often ignored. We all have different bodies and unique histories to our bodies that makes movements and exercise difficult and dangerous if you fail to understand your body.

I had been retired for a period of around seven years and noticed that despite still being in physically good shape I no longer performed any real heart-raising exercise. I would still exercise most days, but it was purely movement I had spent decades doing so my heart and system was not pushed by this approach. So, once a month I began to undertake hard physical cardio type exercise that would stress my heart rate. This was how I achieved an extreme $VO_2$ max level of 74 as a professional athlete (how much oxygen your body can absorb and use during exercise. The higher the figure the better your oxygen uptake). Despite this fact I no longer was that athlete of the past. To try and re-increase my oxygen uptake levels I needed to perform vigorous exercise. Yet I did not want to do this by spending hours working out as I had new and different goals for my own KongDay monitoring. Initially I found I was able to run on a treadmill for 5k, continually attempting faster and faster times. After my body was used to running these 5k sprints I had to switch this to just performing short 30 second – 1-minute sprints at maximum velocity. After this, I found getting into a swimming pool a better way to chase VO$_2$ max.

An unexpected but important development that came from this approach was that this constant changing of exercise caused a level of mental stress that was not reflected in my heart rate. When I was training full-time and multiple times daily this was a side effect from exercise I did not notice. I put it down to just being a fighter that my mental strength was very high. However, it was due to undertaking new movements that are mentally stressful and it was this continually stressing and dealing with adversity that trained my mental state to cope alongside the physical stress.

## Facing stress is good

So, yes, increase your heart and lung capacity but do not underestimate the training of your mind when you are doing this.

*Exercise may be the only outlet we have*
*to embrace suffering by choice.*

The deliberate practice of choosing workouts that stress you mentally is a format you might want to try. The benefits of undertaking such challenges play a key part in ensuring you build a strong mind to hold off other mental challenges. In my own periods of depression, I believe my exercise regime was the crucial reason the depression did not spiral out of control.

Have you suffered from darkened levels in the past and felt depressed?

If so, consider what your physicality routine looked like in those times. It may have been non-existent and perhaps the underlying cause or an addition to what increased the depression.

Current world champion heavyweight boxer Tyson Fury has become the recent poster boy for this stark reality that depression is simply a part of our evolution. In mankind's early history, there was no choice but simply to face taking on dangerous fight or flight scenarios. Although the regular occurrence of wild animal attacks is long gone, we might now need to create our own stressors in a safe but physically demanding arena to help our minds. This is, after all, how meditation and breathing works by calming and relaxing the stress response. Staying balanced is about being able to deal with adversity, so facing adversity can prompt your heart to stressed levels that then induce controlled calming.

Of course, finding a fast treadmill time that pushes you to the max is not comparable to running from a lion but in the internal firings of our system it might not be that different. Could the secret now to help so many mental health challenges be to actually chase small stresses and build resilience rather than trying to avoid any stress in life?

> *"If there is meaning in life at all, then there must be a meaning in suffering. Suffering is an ineradicable part of life, even as fate and death. Without suffering and death, human life cannot be complete."*
>
> Viktor Frankl

Viktor Frankl spent 3 years in concentration camps across Nazi Germany so we should listen when he speaks regarding suffering. Frankl's claim was a necessity to reframe the mind, so one embraces suffering to live a complete life. Most of us, thankfully, do not need to experience the horrors Frankl did so we need to find ways to suffer safely to strengthen our mind. We can't control the extent of suffering we face in life, but the more preparation we include to build our mental toolbox the more likely our mind will be rigorous enough to defeat and deal with it. This is often the huge benefit of sport for children – learning to deal with adversity that to them, in that moment of defeat, spells the end of the world but in the scheme of life is nothing but a small setback they have long conquered.

Despite what you may have been told, mental toughness without doubt improves over time. However, like our brain's plasticity it will start disappearing if you don't put yourself through challenges, no matter how tough you think your mind currently is. Former silver star marine and good friend of mine, Brian Stann, once told me that sometimes he chooses to go without sleep for a night or two. I was astounded by this declaration and couldn't understand why, given how important sleep is and the fact that he was a competitive top ten fighter at the time. His response was that, due to his past and previous years spent in war zones, lack of sleep was a common occurrence. The side-effect he noticed in this state was that he often felt mentally tougher and sharper during and after such episodes. Stann, in his own way, was implementing suffering to receive benefits and in his own words, "to know I still can". Soldiers have reported heightened concentration and focus during sleep deprivation and their lesson may serve as another reason why the non-military amongst us should create similar strategies to prosper.

# Key Implementations:
## Physicality

> Understand that extreme exercise is often unhealthy but conversely plays a role in mental strength training.

> Try as many different types of workouts and movements as you can. Only then will you be more likely to find things you enjoy and stick to.

> Incorporate regular movement into your day, limit the time spent sitting and replicate a toddler's movements where possible.

> Your physicality goal is about working with your heart rate. To improve Vo2 max and fitness levels you will have to train yourself in higher heart rate zones.

# My Physicality Score charts for 2020

Physical - Visual Shades

|     | JAN | FEB | MAR | APR | MAY | JUN | JUL | AUG | SEP | OCT | NOV | DEC |
|-----|-----|-----|-----|-----|-----|-----|-----|-----|-----|-----|-----|-----|
| 1   | 1   | 3   | 4   | 4   | 5   | 3   | 4   | 2   | 3   | 3   | 3   | 2   |
| 2   | 3   | 2   | 5   | 5   | 2   | 3   | 3   | 2   | 3   | 5   | 2   | 5   |
| 3   | 1   | 3   | 2   | 2   | 3   | 2   | 3   | 3   | 3   | 4   | 3   | 5   |
| 4   | 2   | 4   | 2   | 2   | 4   | 3   | 2   | 3   | 4   | 5   | 2   | 4   |
| 5   | 4   | 2   | 4   | 4   | 3   | 4   | 3   | 3   | 3   | 2   | 4   | 4   |
| 6   | 4   | 3   | 3   | 2   | 4   | 4   | 5   | 3   | 1   | 5   | 4   | 4   |
| 7   | 2   | 3   | 2   | 3   | 2   | 5   | 2   | 4   | 3   | 3   | 2   | 4   |
| 8   | 4   | 5   | 4   | 2   | 5   | 4   | 3   | 2   | 5   | 5   | 5   | 2   |
| 9   | 4   | 3   | 5   | 3   | 3   | 4   | 3   | 5   | 4   | 2   | 4   | 5   |
| 10  | 4   | 4   | 2   | 5   | 2   | 4   | 3   | 4   | 5   | 2   | 2   | 4   |
| 11  | 2   | 3   | 2   | 2   | 4   | 5   | 2   | 4   | 3   | 5   | 5   | 5   |
| 12  | 5   | 3   | 3   | 4   | 4   | 3   | 3   | 3   | 1   | 3   | 5   | 4   |
| 13  | 4   | 5   | 4   | 4   | 5   | 4   | 2   | 3   | 5   | 4   | 5   | 5   |
| 14  | 3   | 4   | 2   | 4   | 4   | 3   | 2   | 5   | 5   | 4   | 2   | 4   |
| 15  | 4   | 2   | 3   | 4   | 5   | 3   | 3   | 5   | 4   | 5   | 3   | 4   |
| 16  | 4   | 3   | 3   | 4   | 2   | 4   | 4   | 5   | 5   | 3   | 5   | 4   |
| 17  | 4   | 3   | 2   | 4   | 2   | 5   | 3   | 5   | 5   | 2   | 3   | 4   |
| 18  | 2   | 2   | 3   | 4   | 5   | 4   | 2   | 3   | 3   | 5   | 5   | 3   |
| 19  | 4   | 4   | 2   | 3   | 3   | 3   | 5   | 3   | 3   | 5   | 5   | 4   |
| 20  | 3   | 1   | 3   | 5   | 3   | 4   | 5   | 4   | 3   | 3   | 5   | 4   |
| 21  | 3   | 3   | 2   | 5   | 3   | 5   | 5   | 5   | 3   | 5   | 3   | 5   |
| 22  | 4   | 1   | 2   | 5   | 3   | 3   | 4   | 4   | 3   | 4   | 2   | 3   |
| 23  | 3   | 3   | 1   | 5   | 2   | 4   | 4   | 5   | 3   | 4   | 5   | 4   |
| 24  | 4   | 4   | 5   | 5   | 3   | 2   | 4   | 2   | 2   | 5   | 5   | 5   |
| 25  | 2   | 4   | 4   | 4   | 3   | 4   | 3   | 4   | 5   | 4   | 5   | 2   |
| 26  | 4   | 3   | 5   | 2   | 3   | 2   | 2   | 4   | 5   | 5   | 4   | 1   |
| 27  | 2   | 3   | 4   | 5   | 5   | 4   | 4   | 3   | 5   | 4   | 3   | 3   |
| 28  | 4   | 3   | 2   | 5   | 2   | 4   | 3   | 4   | 5   | 3   | 2   | 3   |
| 29  | 2   | 4   | 4   | 3   | 4   | 2   | 3   | 1   | 5   | 3   | 3   | 4   |
| 30  | 3   |     | 5   | 4   | 3   | 3   | 3   | 4   | 3   | 5   | 5   | 4   |
| 31  | 2   |     | 2   |     | 5   |     | 5   | 3   |     | 2   |     | 4   |

Physical - Year Score Count

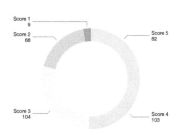

Score 1  
9

Score 2  
68

Score 5  
82

Score 3  
104

Score 4  
103

Physical Score Counts

|         | January | February | March | April | May | June | July | August | September | October | November | December | Total |
|---------|---------|----------|-------|-------|-----|------|------|--------|-----------|---------|----------|----------|-------|
| Score 5 | 1       | 2        | 5     | 9     | 7   | 4    | 5    | 7      | 11        | 12      | 12       | 7        | 82    |
| Score 4 | 14      | 7        | 7     | 11    | 6   | 12   | 7    | 9      | 3         | 7       | 4        | 16       | 103   |
| Score 3 | 6       | 14       | 6     | 4     | 11  | 10   | 12   | 10     | 13        | 7       | 7        | 4        | 104   |
| Score 2 | 9       | 4        | 12    | 6     | 7   | 4    | 7    | 4      | 1         | 5       | 7        | 3        | 68    |
| Score 1 | 2       | 2        | 1     | 0     | 0   | 0    | 0    | 1      | 2         | 0       | 0        | 1        | 9     |

# 5: COGNITION

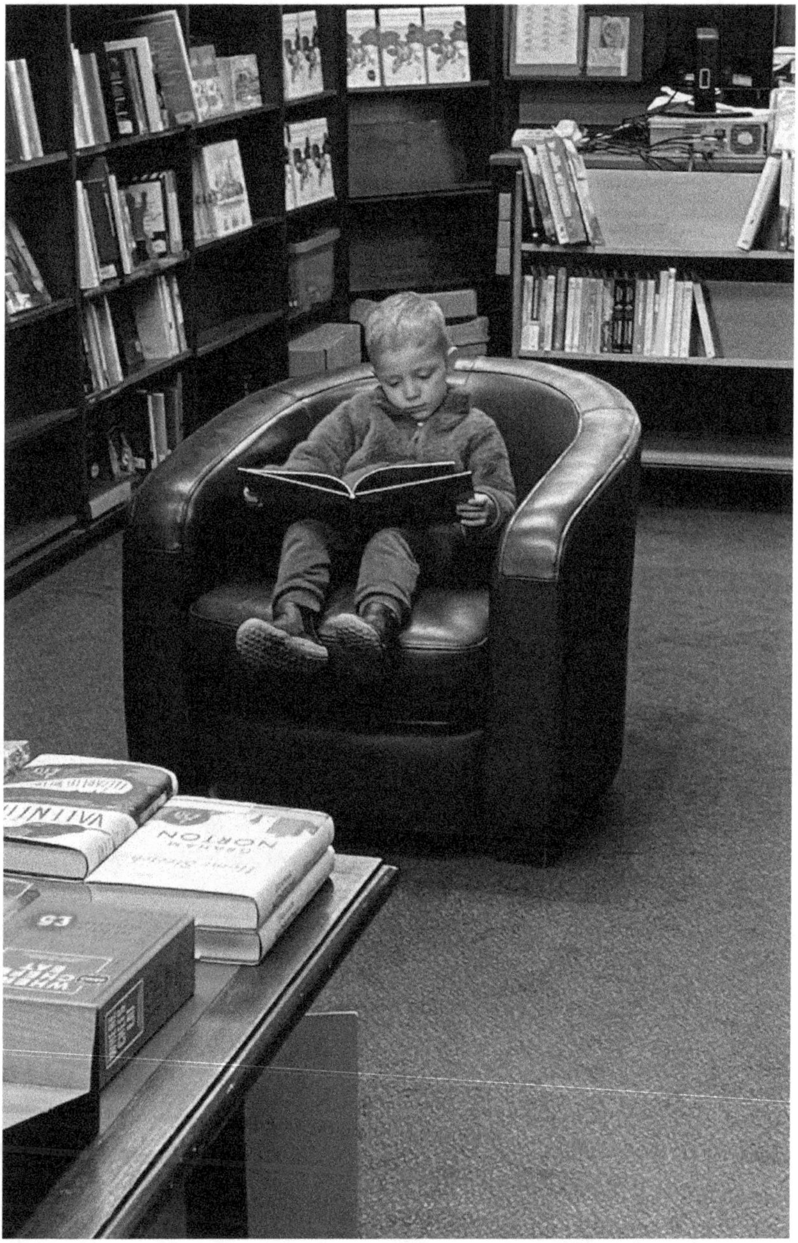

# A cautionary tale

THE TALE OF William James Sidis is not one most will be familiar with. Sidis was an American prodigy who was enrolled at Harvard University from age 11. He was teaching mathematical lectures to professors before graduating at 16. With such proficiency Sidis was touted as a possible new hope for humanity. With knowledge akin to Einstein what secrets might he unlock for the bettering of the human experience? Why haven't we heard of him?

His father, Boris, a renowned Harvard professor, spent a great amount of time *cognitively* training his son to achieve advanced intelligence at the expense of any other variable in life − a lack of KongDay scheduling if you will. With no physical outlets, little regard for nutrition, relationships or sleep, William Sidis broke down as a young adult. Clearly cognitively sharp the diminishing return example again shines through. The cognitive benefit went past a point of increased output. Further, this story is important because it raises an important question central to developing your own cognition strategy, what exactly is intelligence?

Sidis, despite clear academic prowess, showed little intelligence when it came to social interactions and how that might stimulate a brain. After university he spent most of his adult life choosing to work in menial jobs due to a failure to develop a rounded cognition to navigate society. As we look back on school and education, we see there are many holes in how to effectively judge intelligence or teach it. My best friend at school, whom I still speak with now, was in pretty much all the bottom classes and left without a single exam grade. Yet, watching him now organise construction work, I will see him calculate sq meterage, find solutions to engineering dilemmas and manage his environment with ease. There was little place in school for a cognitive intelligence that knew how to deconstruct engines or be adept in social situations.

The key is to remember that intelligence comes in a variety of forms and it is what is important to you that matters. Learning how bricks are laid is still acquiring knowledge, but too often academic snobbery undervalues practical and trade type skills, even though everything is a form of learning to the brain. The reason I want you to consider cognition for your daily behaviour is due to how I have witnessed that most people do not even consider it. They place no emphasis on training their brain as they age. This is not brain training where you sit down to work out puzzles or riddles. Sure, they can play a role in boosting your brain but why limit a key area of our health and development to such a small area? IQ scores are not the goal here (William Sidis registered a higher IQ than Einstein and Stephen Hawking) so what metric do we put forward to monitor our cognitive daily score?

The word cognition describes the act of knowing. Therefore, the more we can 'know' the more we will be improving our cognition score. This brings me to a quote attributed to Socrates:

*"The more I learn, the less I realise I know."*

Socrates

# Go back to basics

Perhaps we should understand that we never really know anything but merely undertake journeys of exploration that lead us through different learnings and experiences. A good starting point then for cognition is to focus (much like mobility for your physical shape) on toddlers. Everything to a toddler is a massive neural explosion. A firing of cells that only begins culling its neurons once something is no longer new. If you want new neurons to fire you need new experiences for the mind.

Numeracy, reading, writing, communication and artistic play are the stable five central areas that form the backbone of cognitive stimuli to this age group. These five areas are just as important to adults' brains, so what can we do to improve in these areas? Maybe start by devoting more time to those areas you feel you are not good at or have long avoided. Poor at maths at school? Start a new plan to learn mathematics, as now there is no pressure from a teacher or exams. Children develop so much because every day is new, and they are faced with so many unknown challenges. Be that child again.

# Try something new

Look at developing new practical skills, for example, learning the art of blacksmithing. For your cognitive brain this now becomes a valuable learning and stimulating environment. The more new stimuli you can encounter, the greater the probability you will find an area you truly enjoy. This happened to me through taking up playing the piano, having never played any music previously. I would make this caveat too for cognitive activities: you should enjoy them as you progress. If you do not enjoy something, how much can it really stimulate your brain?

Developing an unorthodox and creative mindset will also help you develop neurologically. Shake up simple habits. Approaches such as brushing your teeth with the other hand might seem odd, but this is because your neural firing is not as rapid and autonomous as with the usual method. It might not change the structure of your brain, but research shows that even short periods with such interventions do absolutely improve your neural connections. Given that such changes are easy to implement, and dementia charities suggest using them to improve 'brain fitness', they are worth a try.

# Rediscover what you love

Aside from seeking new areas of exploration there is great reward to be had from remembering what it is you already currently love. Cognitive improvement will come from creating time in your daily schedule to rediscover what you love. We all get busy and forget to value the benefit of making sure we satisfy our heart daily. If you do nothing you love, what is the point in being alive? No matter your work or family commitments it is essential you have fun by making sure, without fail, you perform something daily that is just for your soul. This may be a five-minute block for one person or an hour for another. This block is filled with your heart's desire, be it dancing to music, reading, playing music, singing in the shower, kicking a ball – what it is doesn't matter. They all feed your cognitive soul and help make you happier and cognitively better.

Remember, you control your schedule. YOU are the business, so do not listen to the voice that tells you, "But I work for..."

No matter your daily requirements (like taking your kids to school) you must see yourself as the true necessity. To be healthy and sustainable both in the long and short term you need a minimum level of self-satisfaction daily. All work and no play... Start small and take just 5 minutes a day and see how this changes your life. Not just for one day but every single day. The KongDay cognitive mantra is:

*Floss your soul before bed.*

# Design a cognition program

Decide where to begin making changes that will advance your cognitive activity and daily score. The work of James Clear can help us answer this predicament of how best to form habits for cognitive progression. In his bestselling book *Atomic Habits*, Clear details a simple tool to advance your behaviours and make changes. Clear tells us that one of the simplest ways we can form new habits is by making them easy and small to begin with. Let's say we decide to start learning a new language (Mandarin) to improve our cognition. If you begin with a small daily task of just 2 minutes per day you are more likely to keep up with your attempts to learn the language because 2 minutes is easy to find every single day.

We often do the opposite and start our learning journey by scheduling periods that require a lot more time. This soon creates problems, as it's not easy to find 30 minutes (as opposed to 2) to carry on, so we give up. Making it easy to start also silences the mental voice that tells us to give up, as we are not immediately comfortable when learning a new subject. We might tell ourselves we are bad at Mandarin and give up because we tried to advance too quickly. A better approach might look like the following:

You commit to finding 25 minutes a day to put towards cognitive training. You decide to break this up into 5-minute segments as you start, so you can try 5 different cognitive areas. They are:

1. Learn a new language
2. Read fiction
3. Do something artistic
4. Work with numbers
5. Communicate better

These are completely generic and could be tweaked to be 2 instead of 5 or whatever variable you want.

Beginning with a starting exploration, however, gives you a short time focused to each area to decide what you enjoy most and what future time you want to dedicate to continuing. From there, a continued exploration might mean by week 2-3 you may have tried 10-15 new learning concepts and potentially narrowed these down to now just focusing your 30-minute time slot on one area. Now you can work on the daily habit and begin upping your time spent working on this task and in turn upping your cognitive self-score.

# Prove me wrong

I challenge anyone reading this book to contradict my next statement. I've yet to meet any person that is highly competent in a skill with minimal hours spent on the subject. Only those who spend time become highly competent. Often the mindset upon starting a task is as important as the task itself. Positive associations equals better cognitive performance (*Better Mood and Better Performance*, Ruby Nadler, 2010). Just having a better mood when performing tasks improves performance. How much of your attitude then affects your results and behaviours? Ensuring your internal talk is positive is a simple cognition change you can make right now. Silence the negativity.

To develop positive associations, begin by not putting pressure on yourself when starting – simply try to enjoy experiences. Absolutely do not look for feedback too early or judge your skill/ability. I write this because our brain is responsible for the mental feedback loops we play to ourselves. Often these create a worst-case scenario by imagery and visual outcomes. Emily Holmes, professor of clinical psychology at Uppsala University found that people are heavily focusing on the images the mind creates (as opposed to verbal) and changing this dynamic can lead to healing post-traumatic stress disorder. The imagery within your mind is very important to the cognitive health you foster. Search for any methods that work to bring negativity down.

My own experience in combat sports often saw many fighters branded as arrogant or cocky by the general public. The difference was these individuals were attempting to be among the world's greatest competitors and had long figured out that pessimism just makes bad outcomes more likely to occur.

Muhammad Ali was and still is known as the king of self-proclamation, and many have since followed his path.

So, why don't ordinary members of society do the same and implement positive attitudes about future events? A lot of this comes down to society. I was struck, after living in America for a decade, how American society encourages positive emotions and winning at all levels of life. Contrast this with my birthplace of England, which seems to encourage modesty and seeks to put down consistent winning talents or a positive proclamation. In my recollection, as a general observation, American society just seemed happier. Try in your own life to change your responses and attitudes by looking for optimism and positivity. It is quite easy to find someone else to be the negative voice for you, so rather than wait for others to be our positive voice we need to make our own.

## Cultivate the positive

"I'm no good at languages as I can't say any of these Russian words." Neither could anyone in history when they started Russian – they employed patience, using time to develop. That negative inner voice is a hard natural part of the human psyche to fight against, and you can witness young children already demonstrating natural insecurities. However, a little encouragement goes a long way. Upon positive feedback and hearing they are really good at x makes them enjoy the task and want to keep doing it more.

I fell in love with football because early on people told me I was good at it due to practising with the ball a lot. The cycle meant I believed football was natural to me and I would be rewarded with praise. The challenge becomes to find ways, both as children and adults, to persevere with those things we struggle with initially. Only by dedicating time might we find we later experience praise and find new paths. I lost all my first boxing fights and I'm not sure to this day why I carried on. The likelihood is that I felt an internal failure after not becoming a professional footballer. I never wanted to become a professional fighter but after losing repeatedly, giving up would be failing again. If you can find the tenacity to enjoy challenges you will fail at, you will be more likely to seek tasks you won't pass initially. Resilience has then also been cognitively built. The flow state and enjoyment I received once I had mastery in boxing was incredible, keep going and see your proficiency change your experience.

## Don't just 'believe'

This positive mindset approach to me must be distinct from seemingly similar strategies such as those found in *The Secret* by Rhonda Byrnes. This book is hugely popular and describes a law of attraction as fundamental to bringing you everything you have ever wanted, if only you just believe it. As a man of science such a prescription is horrifying and frankly insulting to those that suffer horrendous outcomes as, according to this credo, they must have not believed hard enough. They must take responsibility for whatever tragedy has suddenly occurred in their life. Instead of this, you need to focus on the thought that only work and time spent on tasks will improve your learning and cognition. Fate and life cannot be controlled simply by 'believing', and dreaming is not going to affect reality.

## Create habits

Remember that you must begin by creating a habit to give yourself a better shot at learning and improving. Next, work on your attitude as you undertake the task. I personally used this with my musical learning, by shifting my piano training time to be performed at the end of the day in a small bar I built on the end of my house. Having a small relaxing drink and playing standing up meant the piano was associated with an enjoyment period where I could relax alone. I didn't end up sitting for long periods to improve, so I wasn't worried about adversely affecting my physical goals. Be thorough in your analysis of the best method you could find for that stage of learning. I had to tweak my small glass of red wine which, despite making my start better, later became needing a drink to play music!

Q: What small changes could you make to improve your skill or learning development goals?

_____

_____

_____

_____

_____

_____

# Fighting procrastination

The dreaded procrastinator. It is within us all and we would do well to heed this quote that ties all these areas together:

> *"Men of habits, excellence is a habit."*
>
> Marcus Aurelius

The man in question, Marcus Aurelius, was a Roman emperor and his religion was stoicism. Stoicism was about indifference to responding to that which you cannot change. Aurelius understood that excellence was built by consistent habits and repeating actions regardless of what happened to him that day. His daily routine included self-analysis and he became, with the help of mentors, a master in critiquing his own character and behaviours.

_____

_____

_____

_____

_____

_____

People who schedule and organise are always more successful. Japanese monks begin every day by waking early and immediately cleaning. This is to ensure that a clean and organised approach will be in place as the day progresses. If you can lock down exact times in your schedule when you want to do something, it is more likely to get done. If I force myself every day to perform breathing exercises at 6am for 10 minutes, I won't find myself at the end of the day regretting the fact I missed my goal of breathing meditation. Once you have a solid and unbreakable routine, add some spontaneous behaviour. But I would suggest that this might also be scheduled creative time.

At Google, employees are given daily periods for free-ranging exploration. It is during this creative time that gmail and a host of other technological successes have been developed. This would not have been possible if the entire work schedule had been unstructured, or if it had been totally fixed and rigid. It is a balance of the two. It's one of the very reasons that the richer a person is, the more likely you will find a PA behind the scenes organising their schedule.

This can be a hard task to undertake initially, but with simple steps it can be life-changing. This is the principal reason why I set up KongDay. I am simply showing and reminding people to track and monitor daily habits and actions in crucial areas, every single day. The key to cognitive health then is about becoming organised and getting your time organised. This is the key to success in business. No matter how successful a company becomes, keep improving with defined practice.

## Create structure

Those of you with children know that, from changing nappies to cleaning teeth, putting structure and habits in place makes life easier. Work out your own weekly habitual behaviours. Many probably go unnoticed.

Enter below every daily behaviour you are likely to perform tomorrow:

_____

_____

_____

_____

_____

_____

_____

_____

Make this as in-depth as you can by listing mundane events such as eating to time spent on the toilet. How would the above change if you completed the same but for all the different days of the week. Any different habits to be noted depending on the day?

A personal favourite of mine is many clients noticing how long they spend on the toilet! The culprit being phone scrolling. For one of my female clients this was justified by the toilet being a period of peace and quiet, locked away! Added up over time is this a worthwhile habit and behaviour? Pick your routine apart to find all the areas to omit and what new behaviours you could implement. Have fun designing your new plan and push yourself to include areas that will be cognitively challenging but rewarding if you can make them habitual. I personally went from not reading to reading every day for a minimum of 30 minutes. The pleasure I get from something I never used to do is one of the best rewards KongDay has gave me.

# The optimal path to cognitive success

In searching for expert advice, we would do well to look towards a man who passed away at the time of me writing this chapter, Anders Ericsson. Ericsson was born in Sweden and spent his lifetime studying expert performance. From musicians to chess players, Ericsson attempted to tease out key principles for what behaviours made areas such as medicine and sport advance to the expert level. His work was made famous in popular literature through the likes of Malcom Gladwell in *Outliers* and in *Freakonomics* by Levitt & Dubner. If you take one truth away from the lifetime's work of Ericsson it should be that despite publishing over 300 scientific papers, he could ***never find any evidence to suggest a person is born with an advantage to learn.***

For your cognitive learning I want to relay the best way to progress is determined by an area Ericsson titled as 'Deliberate practice'. This occurs just beyond one's comfort zone. Too far behind your current skill level and the task is too hard to gain maximum improvements. Too easy and there is too little stimulation to sufficiently progress. There is a worldwide notion of 10,000 hours to become a master. *Outliers* botched Ericsson's theory to define the clock as 10,000 hours. Ericsson never mentioned 10,000 hours directly but brought attention to an idea that to make the elite level, musicians needed to amass roughly around 10,000 hours of practice as a minimum. This miscommunication spurred a host of people into concluding that 10,000 hours of practice meant you would become elite. What this missed was the importance of how these 10,000 hours are spent. Gladwell himself also recently expressed regret in a podcast with Adam Grant stating that his 10,000 hour message does not hold true. If you can master deliberate practice routines a person might bring this number down to far less hours.

# Using 10,000 hours

Dan McLaughlin was a photographer who quit his job to begin a new schedule, one that dedicated 10,000 hours to becoming a world class golf pro. Called *The Dan Plan* and accredited to Gladwell, McLaughlin adopted it having had no previous experience of golf (sounds like my MMA journey!). The challenge was dedicating 30-plus hours a week to master golf despite being in his thirties. This could be achieved after 6+ years of 30-hour practice weeks to reach 10,000 hours. Dan did get down to an impressive 2 handicap but never achieved his goal of professional golf mastery. Clearly, after all that time spent, Dan had become a very good golfer, but to be a great one, the key requisite was missing, that of 'deliberate practice'.

All the musicians in Ericsson's research logged over 10,000 hours but that was not the true causality to who became the best. Ericsson found that was due to those in the group who spent more time in deliberate practice states, some even practised for fewer hours than the others. It is essentially the quality of your hours rather than just hours logged. Most of you are not going to dedicate 30 hours a week towards new regimes but the more time you can find the better, but focus on the deliberate practice zone. This is found when a task is not too hard or too easy because that is the place you are challenged just beyond your comfort level. The more you practise then the more you need to increase difficulty. This is why you must become self-analytical in your journey, using methods such as journalling to review and constantly upgrade the nature of your practice.

## Achieving flow state

Deliberate practice puts people into a zone sometimes referred to as flow state, where you practise in a state of flow. It takes a while to achieve this state as no beginner has competency to enter a flowing movement pattern. As a competitive fighter I could not often remember many of the details directly after fights. I would enter such a trance state that many matches were like an out of body experience. I would feel as if I was watching myself compete, with somebody else controlling my movements. This only happened after many years of championship fights. Ericsson, before he died, published the book *Peak: Secrets from the New Science of Expertise* which I would encourage you to read to help you in realising your own individual goals. Maybe look toward areas that have always interested you, but you've never actually got around to trying. Once you begin it may not be long with consistent time to get nearer to a flow state practice. For me, I have used Ericsson's methodology to improve my language learning. Sick of internalising the words "I wish I could speak another language" I decided to implement Ericsson's advice and seek a flow state in language. This became possible after consistent daily practice and a habit of reading Spanish texts aloud. By using this approach I would find I would look at the clock and notice I had been speaking Spanish for 20 minute periods, flowing my words.

# Circulatory factors to stall and reverse brain ageing

In looking at cognitive health, we need to return to diet and lifestyle as key aspects which contribute to the process of healing a brain and being able to continually cognitively perform.

Remember genetics. In how we age, genetics is only 20-30% of the causality, with the remaining 60-70% down to environmental factors. My old appearance is the product of over 100 fights, not simply my genetics. You must check your environment. How much time do you spend in nature? How often do you drink or smoke? With the body being made up of water how much are you drinking daily? Is this changing with activity and temperature level changes?

We have mentioned diet and I have seen a young MMA student of mine fail blood pressure medicals despite exercising regularly. With the wrong nutrients, fat deposits increase and the cells, including the brain, will struggle. Therefore, plasticity and brain repair/protection are surely linked to nutrition. What does your diet do for your cellular inflammation? Start viewing food as a necessity to feed your desires and not simply your stomach.

A sci-fi scenario of receiving blood infusions from younger donors is happening. Faecal transplants from healthy individuals also are being used to improve bodily decline of the microbiome and gut. Why not try and get your system fueled optimally now before you end up needing such drastic intervention?

# The most complex part of the human body

Our vessel of being, the brain, is a remarkable thing. As Bill Bryson brilliantly states in his book *The Body*, our brain is a hungry organ. It takes up just 2% of our body weight but requires 20% of its energy. However, before you justify any nutrition on that basis, it can satisfy this remarkable need from only 400 calories daily and also run for longer periods without any input. There is simply no other system of such complexity anywhere else in the body. From all your behaviours to any movement, the brain is the source of all human progress. The importance of these statements makes me tell clients to dedicate more time to cognitive than all the other areas.

Forget working out, instead find 10% of your daily time to stimulate your brain directly. Reading, speaking, listening and moments in thought all become key. Sadly, we do not dedicate 10%, nearly 3 hours daily, to immersive brain behaviour. After decades of neglect in this routine we cannot be surprised that in later life so many suffer. We are limited at present by not being able to clearly regenerate the brain. Other organisms such as an octopus which has 9 brains or a leech with 32 classified brains might provide clues for humans as to how to achieve this but as yet there is nothing of hope. We can regrow liver cells but nothing as significant yet for healing our brain.

For me as a former competitive fighter this is clearly something of a wake-up call. As a young athlete you know the risks and accept the dangers, but it wasn't until much later in my career that one day I began to research older former legendary boxers and document what they were doing now. From my research I compiled a list which showed death being most common once they reached their 50s onwards. These once-champions' last days were often spent in care homes battling dementia or pugilistic dementia (now more commonly known now as CTE, chronic traumatic encephalopathy).

Many other sports have also joined this sad post-sporting club. Jeff Astle, former England and World Cup-winning footballer brought the attention of this disease to the football audience and has caused the Football Association to admit more work needs to be done to help the many ex-players suffering. Footballers have been classed as three times more likely than the general population to suffer from dementia and it should make you wonder if sports need to be updated and changed for protection of unnecessary damage to arguably our most vital organ.

It is not only me that should be concerned. You, reading this book, will be affected. Neurodegeneration affects more than fighters. With the number of people aged 60 and over worldwide set to double in the next 30 years many more will be diagnosed with dementias and Parkinson's. Many of you will then be of that age. *Forget paying into your pension. What are your actions for your brain health now that mean your pension is worth drawing?* Without trying, many of us will become a burden to the people we were once the hero. The brain, like the body, does not age well. You must start working on it every single day. By doing this you will also level up your skill and life experience. Double win.

I have begun my own self-testing brain research that involves going for an MRI scan every 5 years. Having already had 3 over 15 years I have data to document the changes to white/gray matter over the course of my life. Notable for me was a key change between a scan from 2012 when I first entered the UFC and again in 2019 after I had finished competing. The 2019 scan showed a black line that was determined as a potential former bleed or stress from contact, absorbed in those additional 5 years. Having this information changed my future and daily approach towards my brain health and ultimately stopped me competing. It was time for a new change in life. If any of my future scans have any positive findings, I would be able to pair these with all my individual data collected in KongDay and see what habits and nutritional strategies might be usable by others. The systemic environment is different for all of us, and supplementation would play a factor but there are already hopes and methods we can currently use for our own cognitive programming.

# The value of journalling

For most of my life I have never journalled. I began the practice after hearing about a person in my local area of a similar age who had died suddenly. The correct advice most people receive is to take out life insurance and have your affairs in order, to leave less burden to those left if disaster strikes. Again, many of us fail to do this because we will get round to it another day. I also became focused on the problem of what my early death would mean to my young son, what would he know about his father? If most of us look back, we do not really have many memories from a young age. We might have some snapshots or images we have created but otherwise it tends to be at secondary school age and beyond that we have detailed recollections. I decided that one of the best heirlooms I could pass along would be a daily journal about my thoughts and interactions. I thought that at some point this would provide an insight to my son about who his father was. I then imagined being able to read memoirs of my dad's father and beyond that, his grandfather etc. Having this motivation has made the process of journalling easier because I commit to a reason for doing it daily. It will be my unique legacy to my bloodline and beyond, the thoughts and happenings of my time.

The negative effect sometimes seen in journalling is that, by recounting it, we can heighten the negative effect of a painful emotional experience. Further, this might then increase not decrease a worsening of the immune system.

I have found the best success comes from merely documenting your day without regard for deep meaning. It is easy to do and on days the writing takes you, you can add experiences and write more as you progress. Remember back to the suggestion that most habits are firstly concerned with forming the habit before adding complexity. In your first attempts you will miss days and struggle to know what to write. I do not believe there is an optimal length of time. My initial journalling was laborious in that I kept forgetting to do it rather than struggling for time. It was two months before journalling was something I reached to do daily as a habit before bed and I will still occasionally forget to make an entry.

I use an A5 notepad and for me, I just don't do it daily if it's not handwritten. However, of course you may choose to journal on an electronic device as many of my clients do. This book lays out the benefits of adopting the KongDay system, and throughout the book you are encouraged to make notes and answer questions on the page. If you use this book to make your own notes and journal scribbles it will get you started on the path to holistic self development. On a holistic self learning experience that journalling brings. With clients I encourage them to find a 'page a day diary' that are often for sale cheaply and make this their more detailed journal for reviewing and advancing KongDay.

> *Journalling is one of the first changes I ask new KongDay users to incorporate into their lives.*

This is because journalling is one of the simplest ways to begin learning and reflecting about yourself and your actions. Almost all of us looking back with affection at those social media time hop photo memories, and, in the same way, re-reading journal entries can be another great way to relive emotions and experiences. It will help you to assess your changing character and lifestyle as you move forward.

I have also used journalling for additional cognitive challenges and gains. I set myself the task in January 2020 to only writing in the journal left-handed as shown across. After 42 days, my handwriting was legible, but my writing pace was still very slow. I continued and found that after around 6 months my left hand was equal to my right hand in writing. I believe this experience of using my left hand in writing has made other activities like playing the piano easier due to being more comfortable with both hands. Watching people who have lost limbs and learn to paint with their feet shows that perhaps the only limitation is believing you have mastered the only way to perform something.

Sleep - 6.5 - Woke up 5 am

## 2 Thursday

week 1 (002-364)

Bank Holiday - Scotland

8.00 The benefits of journalling! Usually get nothing done, woke up and did
9.00 meditation 15 mins and Spanish. Any day so probably wouldn't get it done otherwise. Bring a book everywhere to
10.00 as never seem to learn as much watching or reading on phone. Pick up
11.00 big piano session when back to recover gaps.

12.00

Amazing night with Dave P at Anfield.
1.00 So privileged to be able to live how I do & have inspirational ppl around me like him.
2.00 Brain tumour but always positive. Be more pavarotti. I find it hard to watch Santi
3.00 eating rubbish but lead by example thats it.

4.00 C-3, S-2, P 3, R 5, N-4, B-3

5.00 OPT score of 20! - V. good for being away. keep it

December '19      Notes      up.
Su Mo Tu We Th Fr Sa
1  2  3  4  5  6  7

# The habit of reading

If there is one practice most would associate with long-term brain health, it would be reading. This simple practice allows a period of concentrated focus that can mentally transform the brain to visualise new experiences and faraway lands. Reading and written text has been the best way to pass knowledge through generations. Consider the following:

> *"The written word has the magical power of transforming thoughts from one person's brain into another's. Over distance and time. As a teenager I realised that in books I could access the brains of the smartest people in the world. Even those who were dead. I could tap into years of learning in just a few hours. This felt like a superpower. It still does."*
>
> Ev Williams (co-founder of twitter and CEO of Medium).

At least half of all the clients I have worked with state that they don't read. The figure seems to be rising. The reasoning is that they can't absorb information or enjoy it but I feel this is due to society now finding far easier ways to stimulate the brain. Please try to encourage others to get into reading by perhaps gifting books and discussing the benefits. As someone reading my book I likely do not have to convince you of the power of the written word.

# Key Implementations:
## Cognition

> Make topics challenging but not too hard. This is where the flow state or deliberate practice zone exists. You will learn and progress further in this zone.

> Pick topics initially that are outside your normal behaviour and interest. Try more than once before giving up.

> Seek experts at the beginning of any journey and where possible search and pay for a masterclass entry experience.

> Start ensuring you dedicate time daily to floss your brain through laughter, play and creative exploration.

> Make any changes small to start with and then slowly increase your daily time spent learning.

> Journal every day, no matter the quality or quantity.

# My Cognition Score charts for 2020

Cognitive - Visual Shades

| | JAN | FEB | MAR | APR | MAY | JUN | JUL | AUG | SEP | OCT | NOV | DEC |
|----|-----|-----|-----|-----|-----|-----|-----|-----|-----|-----|-----|-----|
| 1 | 3 | 4 | 3 | 4 | 4 | 2 | 4 | 2 | 2 | 3 | 4 | 2 |
| 2 | 3 | 4 | 3 | 4 | 3 | 1 | 4 | 3 | 2 | 4 | 4 | 3 |
| 3 | 2 | 3 | 3 | 4 | 4 | 3 | 5 | 4 | 1 | 3 | 4 | 3 |
| 4 | 3 | 3 | 4 | 3 | 3 | 4 | 4 | 3 | 2 | 3 | 2 | 2 |
| 5 | 3 | 3 | 3 | 3 | 4 | 2 | 4 | 2 | 3 | 3 | 3 | 4 |
| 6 | 4 | 3 | 2 | 3 | 3 | 3 | 3 | 2 | 2 | 3 | 2 | 3 |
| 7 | 4 | 3 | 3 | 3 | 3 | 3 | 3 | 2 | 1 | 3 | 3 | 4 |
| 8 | 3 | 3 | 3 | 3 | 3 | 4 | 4 | 2 | 2 | 2 | 3 | 3 |
| 9 | 4 | 3 | 3 | 4 | 3 | 4 | 3 | 3 | 4 | 1 | 3 | 2 |
| 10 | 4 | 4 | 4 | 4 | 4 | 4 | 4 | 3 | 3 | 3 | 3 | 3 |
| 11 | 4 | 3 | 3 | 4 | 3 | 2 | 2 | 2 | 2 | 3 | 4 | 4 |
| 12 | 4 | 2 | 3 | 4 | 4 | 4 | 2 | 3 | 1 | 3 | 3 | 3 |
| 13 | 4 | 2 | 3 | 3 | 3 | 2 | 2 | 3 | 3 | 2 | 5 | 3 |
| 14 | 4 | 3 | 2 | 5 | 4 | 3 | 2 | 3 | 3 | 3 | 2 | 4 |
| 15 | 4 | 3 | 3 | 3 | 3 | 3 | 4 | 3 | 3 | 2 | 2 | 3 |
| 16 | 4 | 2 | 3 | 4 | 4 | 4 | 3 | 3 | 3 | 2 | 3 | 3 |
| 17 | 3 | 3 | 2 | 4 | 3 | 4 | 4 | 4 | 3 | 1 | 1 | 2 |
| 18 | 3 | 3 | 2 | 4 | 4 | 4 | 3 | 2 | 3 | 3 | 4 | 1 |
| 19 | 4 | 4 | 3 | 4 | 3 | 5 | 3 | 2 | 4 | 4 | 4 | 3 |
| 20 | 4 | 2 | 3 | 4 | 4 | 2 | 4 | 2 | 3 | 4 | 4 | 3 |
| 21 | 3 | 2 | 3 | 4 | 3 | 3 | 3 | 3 | 2 | 4 | 3 | 3 |
| 22 | 3 | 2 | 3 | 4 | 5 | 2 | 4 | 4 | 3 | 2 | 3 | 3 |
| 23 | 3 | 3 | 3 | 4 | 4 | 4 | 3 | 1 | 3 | 1 | 4 | 2 |
| 24 | 3 | 2 | 3 | 4 | 4 | 3 | 3 | 2 | 4 | 3 | 3 | 2 |
| 25 | 4 | 3 | 3 | 4 | 4 | 4 | 2 | 3 | 1 | 4 | 4 | 2 |
| 26 | 4 | 3 | 4 | 4 | 4 | 2 | 4 | 4 | 3 | 5 | 4 | 3 |
| 27 | 5 | 3 | 3 | 4 | 4 | 3 | 4 | 4 | 4 | 2 | 3 | 4 |
| 28 | 3 | 3 | 3 | 4 | 4 | 4 | 2 | 4 | 4 | 2 | 2 | 5 |
| 29 | 3 | 3 | 3 | 4 | 2 | 4 | 4 | 3 | 5 | 2 | 3 | 4 |
| 30 | 4 | | 3 | 4 | 4 | 3 | 4 | 3 | 4 | 3 | 4 | 3 |
| 31 | 4 | | 4 | | 5 | | 2 | 3 | | 3 | | 3 |

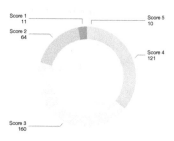

Cognitive - Year Score Count

Score 1 — 11
Score 2 — 64
Score 3 — 160
Score 4 — 121
Score 5 — 10

Cognitive Score Counts

| | January | February | March | April | May | June | July | August | September | October | November | December | Total |
|---------|---------|----------|-------|-------|-----|------|------|--------|-----------|---------|----------|----------|-------|
| Score 5 | 1 | 0 | 0 | 1 | 2 | 1 | 1 | 0 | 1 | 1 | 1 | 1 | 10 |
| Score 4 | 16 | 4 | 4 | 22 | 16 | 12 | 14 | 6 | 6 | 5 | 11 | 5 | 121 |
| Score 3 | 13 | 18 | 23 | 7 | 12 | 9 | 9 | 14 | 12 | 14 | 12 | 17 | 160 |
| Score 2 | 1 | 7 | 4 | 0 | 1 | 7 | 7 | 10 | 7 | 8 | 5 | 7 | 64 |
| Score 1 | 0 | 0 | 0 | 0 | 0 | 1 | 0 | 1 | 4 | 3 | 1 | 1 | 11 |

# 6: RELATIONSHIPS

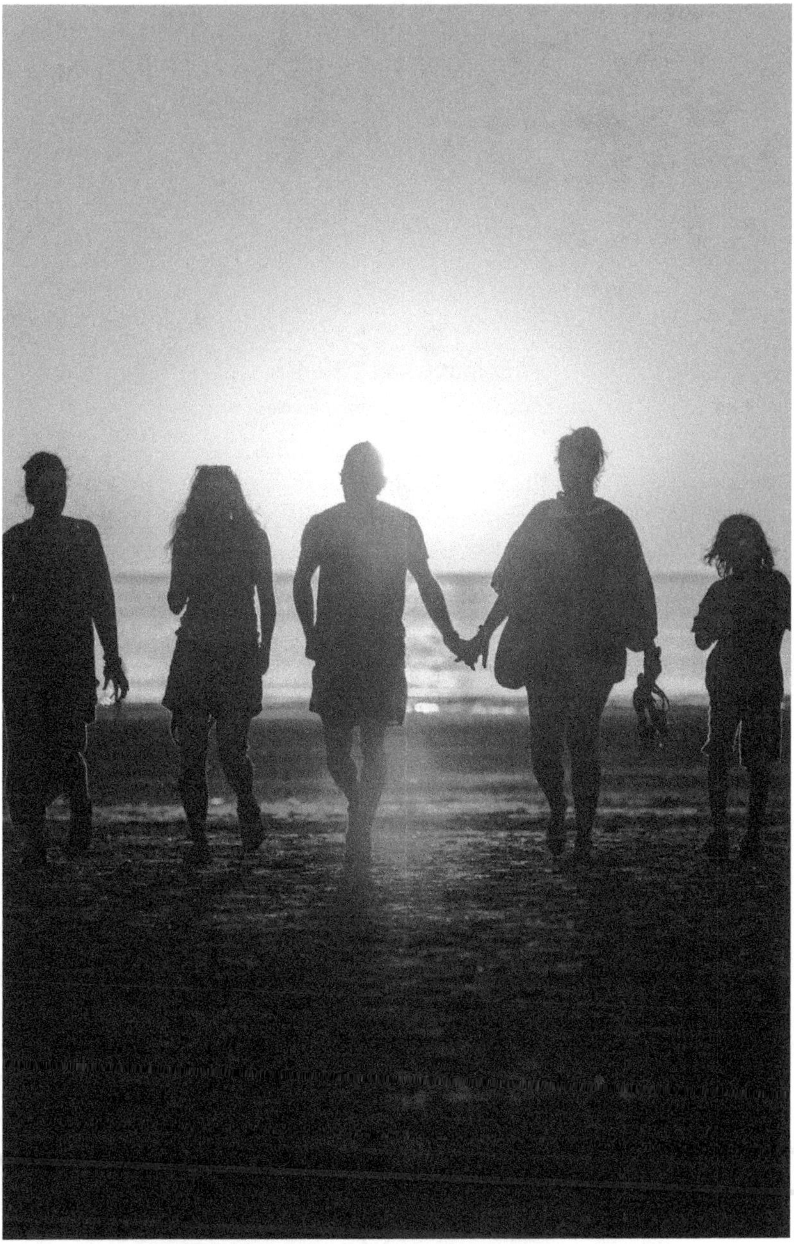

EINSTEIN DECLARED IMAGINATION as more important than knowledge, but was less famous for the following quote:

> *"Some men spend a lifetime in an attempt to comprehend the complexities of women. Others have preoccupied themselves with somewhat simpler tasks, such as understanding the theory of relativity."*
>
> Albert Einstein

Einstein's comedic pondering leads us nicely into the fifth area of the game we should strive to focus upon, relationships.

As alluded to by the genius, improving the relationships around you is nowhere near as easy as many modern-day gurus will prescribe.

I view relationships as the exterior of the cake. So far, we have worked on all the ingredients but only relationships will make the cake stand out. Every interaction to your brain is a relationship. Your mind makes sense of communication and interactions. All experience on earth has formulated the ecosystem to not only the billions of humans but the complete multitude of species that share the planet. Beyond that we are made from stardust, as elements of the human body were originally made in the stars. Helping to understand the expansive nature of our lives can be a great way to release the pressure many feel in the direction their life has taken. Fear not because everything will pass.

We essentially have two crucial interactions to solve. The first being us. We need to master ourselves as that is what interacts with the second area, everything else! I love a quote from Jim Rohn that tells people they are the average of the 5 people they spend the most time with. David Burkus has taken this further with his book *Friend of a Friend* that says it is bigger than those 5. People always look to improve their close family relationships but forget that their interactions with others often have a bigger effect upon them. We may well spend more time with work colleagues than with family so what we do, see and absorb with them forges our mind and our behaviour more than we realise. If we are all honest, all our happiness depends on relationships. From the people around us to the extent of our relationship to the objects we may love, be it a piano or a barbell, everything is a relationship. Reading books is not only a cognitive experience but a relationship development in shaping your character by the words you absorb.

In his Ted talk (https://youtu.be/rPh3c8Sa37M) Tom Chi (an astrophysical researcher, Fortune 500 consultant and part of the founding team for Google X) discusses this interconnected nature of our world. Chi informs people that they possess a 'palette of being' with which they paint. What has existed determines the colour available and every action we take matters somewhere, both in the past and for the future. Our actions will create new colours others can use in their palette of being. I can play the piano only because in 1700 someone made the concept possible, before then it didn't exist. How you affect others is much like early single-celled organisms that didn't see their role in our existence. We are simply unaware of the effect we are having somewhere. Be it direct or indirect.

Chi's movement then calls for a responsibility to enrich the colours from which future generations can paint from. I believe this is how we should strive to approach our relationships. Every action we take is significant, but we often live with only short-term considerations. KongDay is built to have daily actions that satisfy the short-term but also guarantee your long-term health. Reminding yourself of this after uttering some regrettable words can change the nature of future relationships. We can't be perfect and nor should we be robotic in our behaviours, but we can accept that analysing our relationships and working to score them daily might be a way to create a better, more enjoyable world to live in.

# Relationship effects

The work of Nicholas Christakis and James Fowler into relationships in the modern age is truly groundbreaking. They have found that obesity is causal to a person's social networks. They showed that by having one obese friend you become 57% more likely to become obese yourself. Similarly, a sibling becoming obese can make you 40% more likely to become obese and a partner equated to a 37% increase.

These are massive percentage numbers. Think about it. With modern society most of us will have an obese friend or be one, which makes us more likely than not to also become obese if we aren't! The authors and I do not advocate cutting off those in your circle who become/or are obese but highlight the subtle interactive effects we have on each other. Social networks such as Facebook are forming the new way much of our relationships occur. Many people are now put in bad moods just from online interactions. Christakis has also shown that happy and unhappy people cluster together in the same pattern of behaviour as obesity. Leading by example rather than dictating is the only real way I have seen that helps others make changes. We are more likely to implement a 'do as you see' approach rather than 'do as I say'.

Consider your influences now by returning to Jim Rohn and his famous quote, "We are the average of the five people we spend the most time with".

Q: List your current five people below and see what that reveals to you:

1. _____

2. _____

3. _____

4. _____

5. _____

Pairing this advice with Christakis and Fowler, we don't need to cut off relationships, but we should consider that our behaviour is heavily linked to the above people. In the past I have looked at my own 5 people and made changes. Spending a long time in the fight game, it was easy for me to be surrounded by criminals. Despite them not asking me to enter that world, most of my top 5 were formed from this world and my actions and beliefs were influenced, leading to a different world view and resulting life.

This is no different to current online algorithms: after watching an online video you will be fed more reflecting the same ideological interests. We fall deeper and deeper into set beliefs with little thought. Of course, many of you will say that you do not want to change your inner circle. All I want to highlight is to be aware of the influence the 5 will play on your goals and actions.

If you currently can't play the guitar and dream of doing so exceptionally in 10 years, *the people around you will matter*. If your closest circle included some of the greatest guitarists and musical minds, subconsciously you become a different person and would become far more likely to learn and master the guitar. This is how mentoring works. The people you spend the most time with is an influence you have control over. No matter how odd something may seem to outsiders, those within the group can get slowly indoctrinated. Cult killings like that of Jim Jones and the People's Temple in Indiana saw 909 people in 1978 become convinced to drink cyanide. This isn't a one-off. Cults still occur today and kill many people through changing the views of the group. If you have time and a strong stomach, do some research into groups such as 'The Children of God' which still exist today (interestingly a famous actor was born into its values before escaping).

# Find mentors online

The truth to remember is that your 5 people most influential people do not have to all be physical interactions of people you know. I am amazed now that people are unaware of the many ways you can spend more time with great masters and minds. Want to cook? You can easily make Gordon Ramsey one of your top

5 people (without stalking him down and forcing him to spend his time with a stranger) due to hundreds of hours of online material. It is no different for the arts or almost any subject. This is all I did in MMA (Mixed Martial Arts) after suffering a few losses. I asked myself who was the best in the world. I found them in the USA and studied what I could until I could get myself shadowing them daily in the same living environment. I travelled to Canada, Brazil, Thailand and Holland in the same quest. It was easy and it becomes easier every day thanks to technology.

You can produce the excuse that you weren't born with the right situation or genetic gifts, but enlightening mentors are available all around us. Only upon searching might you find that your neighbour is an expert and a world class master in something. Gary Kasparov is a world-famous chess grandmaster, and he can become your mentor for hours a day if that is your ambition. It will cost you roughly only £10 a month using masterclasses and YouTube and whatever information you can source online. You are also getting the very best edited version of Kasparov, not him waking on a bad day telling you to go away.

# What are your life goals?

To forge relationships, most of us will be bound by our goals in life. Some may have buried childhood dreams while others may be in full pursuit of clear current objectives. Robert Waldinger, in his Ted talk *What Makes a Good Life*, details how he searched to answer this question. He began by asking this question to young adult participants: What is your most important life goal?

*80% answered to get rich, 50%*
*said to become famous.*

We can laugh at these young adults and view it as a misunderstanding of life at that age but even if we might be older and wiser do we feel different? I would argue that many older participants still feel internally the same, dreaming of that life-changing experience which money or fame would bring. There might be less chance to become rich or famous as you age but plenty of 'older' people still spend their lives working as hard as possible to maybe achieve extreme wealth or even fame.

Robert Waldinger's research has continued to examine if this is really what we should want or need for our lives. How much would your relationships change if you were famous or extremely rich? I have been someone famous within the MMA world, headlining stadiums, signing autographs and making hundreds of thousands of dollars in minutes. Fame leaves faster than Elton John's candle and before it's gone it wasn't very real anyway.

Interestingly, Waldinger's study has now been continuing for 75 years. Albeit largely men, 724 people have been the focus of a Harvard study into adult development and happiness. 60 of these men are still alive today and report regularly to the study. 2000 of their children and family members have since entered the study, potentially uncovering genetic predispositions. The participants within the study have ranged from a US president to those struggling with schizophrenia. Despite this eclectic mix a clear result has emerged:

*Happiness is related to the quality*
*of your relationships*

So, let's now get to the three big ways we can improve our relationships.

# Start journalling

We have already highlighted the cognitive benefits of journalling but for improving and sustaining relationships, journalling can play a similarly vital role.

Journalling could be the most important habit you need to make daily to improve your relationships. Start by figuring out the best timing and style of journalling that helps make your relationships improve. I found that writing a quick assessment of my relationship behaviour after lunchtime daily gave me an incentive to use time periods later in the day for positive interactions.

C-4, P-2, R-5, S-5, B-5, N-3   (24)

What have you added to for the ... in 1st 2021?

What have I achieved? Achieved is a different world, one I ... usually all associate with Status, ... from others. Two old ... partners compete tonight for the UFC and I often see it advertised now in the ... I want to reason how that was me, everyone seems to have forgotten, was that an achievement? I lived, for a time at ... signing autographs being a champion, being famous but it counts for nothing. The achievement was though my ... mastery of mind & body to think I ... ... daily while I can. I ... to ... down & ... & always want to be somewhere else or someone different, but any achievement so far is this, I'm still here, living & feeling the power & beauty of the ... life. Each moment plus to ... I can catch a few that the best achievement I ever made.

Writing about your emotions and experiences of the day is helpful at the end of the day but you then sleep and start afresh tomorrow. Consider drawing attention earlier to your key relationship behaviours and do something about it before the day ends. This practice has meant I will more often than before find the time to make phone calls or express my love for people close to me than when I did not journal. I also encourage clients to document positive emotions. Write down words you might want to say to your partner or loved ones but don't. It is a lot easier to begin by journalling in a place where you know only you will see the words. Progress can then be made to say these out loud in future meetings. In a worst-case scenario your journal writings might serve as a message should you die, as I have already written. If you are concerned that I keep discussing death fear not because this is a concept that should not be alarming. Your possible reaction to it is crucial for healthy relationships and I will dedicate a complete area below on the importance as to why.

Gratitude is also a central key to encourage in journalling. Forcing yourself to search daily for reasons to be thankful is important, as naturally we miss many simple reasons for gratitude. We all receive enough free negativity so we can use all the good vibes we can get, even if it's via self-created 'love thyself' messages. Marcus Aurelius approves:

> ***"Never be overheard complaining,***
> ***not even to yourself."***
>
> Marcus Aurelius

By not complaining you are training the mind to not reinforce or compound earlier grievances. Another tip might be to document experiences that you wish you could have handled differently. Perhaps you left a conversation questioning why you said x or why you didn't say y. Write down what you would have wished to occur, your fantasy z response. This usually occurs with friends/colleagues rather than loved ones, but journalling again acts as a method to polish up your real-life conversational moments. Journalling is a safe environment in which to improve the way you can express yourself, leading to all sorts of benefits in business and in your relationships.

# Try meditation

Learning about our world and our relationship to it is best done by deep concentrated study. To do so, we need to learn to sit quietly. Nowadays adults and children cannot sit with their own thoughts as the noise of society prevents such quiet contemplation. We are bombarded by pings from devices and the relentless media giving us dopamine hits that forces us to run from silence.

To escape all this, we need to meditate. Meditation is at its core not concerned with chasing the thoughts of past and future actions. Silence gives you the chance to listen to the thoughts inside your head NOW, hear the breathing of your body (compare running to when you run with headphones). We are the only person who lives inside our heads and our world. We need to listen to ourselves, and meditation or silent breathing are excellent ways to achieve this. As with journalling there are many useful meditation apps and courses which you can work through, but it can be found in many ways. A client of mine uses long swimming sessions to enter their meditative state.

# The power of gratitude

Think about your immediate partner if you have one. Our expectations of them go up the longer we are together. When you first meet you might have hopes and dreams and, to stick together, you strive to find the positives over the negatives. If you had concentrated on negatives from the start, then the relationship would not have gone anywhere. However, the longer we are together we seem by familiarity to forget the earlier positives we saw in our partners due to increasing expectations.

Q: Write down 3 things you love about your partner (substitute for a family/friend if you wish)

1. _____

2. _____

3. _____

The more we can take a step back and look at each other with satisfaction rather than expectation the healthier you will find your outlook. We are familiar with people who seem to be extremely content and happy with their life. We might often wonder why they can be so happy, and yet we aren't.

My father has never taken a day off work, does the same thing every day, doesn't buy things, rarely goes anywhere outside of his county (let alone country). My mother on the other hand will see a usual year spent visiting a host of places worldwide. Currently she is travelling across Australia and Singapore and enriches her life with many different experiences daily, yet my father is far more content and arguably happier than my mother. I am not writing this to advocate that we should seek to choose my father's path, far from it, but we should give ourselves a daily reminder and habitual check that expresses gratitude to ensure our experiences and relationships are not constantly judged with tougher eyes.

I lived for over a decade as a professional athlete, on the road alone or surrounded only by teammates. The sacrifices made to try and reach the summit meant I could be in a picturesque Montreal winter but sat alone in an apartment. I had to surround myself with higher level athletes to reach the highest level but looking back, I neglected to spend time working on relationships and missed many experiences and paths that would have led my life to different levels. I should have left Montreal fluent in French but instead I do not speak a word. Do not be angry at what mistakes you have made but accept that only when you create routines and relationship-meaning will you develop your character towards the chance of happier future times. *What is the point in making mistakes if we do not learn from them?*

## The value of feedback

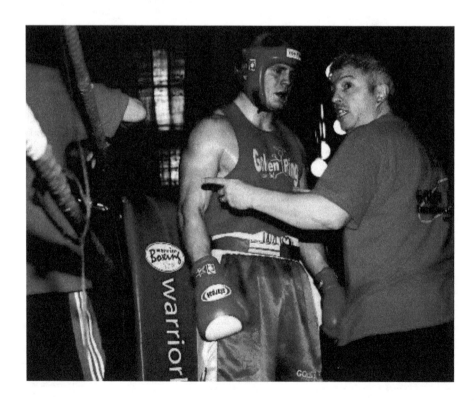

An area where mentors can make a key difference to advancement is in giving effective feedback. Much to my annoyance, my wife will correct my Spanish mistakes but without expert feedback the mistakes go unnoticed. Most of us accept the use of feedback as a tool to increase our learning, so why not apply the same principle to improve your relationships? The challenge becomes getting valuable feedback about ourselves and our character traits from others who see us closely. I recommend choosing 2+ people important to your life and asking them to answer, with complete honesty, the following:

1. Define my worst trait
2. How can I listen/help you more?

If necessary, try and acquire the information randomly to provide anonymity. This helps to avoid any anger or resentment at the answers! While these questions are both negative it is something I would encourage you to do. In competitive sports the best coaches are often brutally honest about performance. In this example we are making others around us the experts, as they will know your traits better than anyone else.

Q: Analyse deeply your relationships and your behaviours. What three things (answering honestly!) would improve them?

_____

_____

_____

_____

_____

_____

_____

_____

# Let's talk about death

A relationship we don't usually want to think about is death. We will all experience it yet most of us don't have any idea how to process and improve our relationship to it. It is truly an uncomfortable and awful event to consider deeply. Modern society goes out of its way to avoid the subject. I can remember as a little boy having long periods of time struggling to get my head around the idea of death. As I got older, I began to understand that the magical children's world was not all as it seemed. Where were my grandparents? Where did they go? I don't want to die.

This fear of death (thanatophobia) is clearly a good thing to possess, as it is a mechanism to keep us alive, but only if we can stop the anxious panic that occurs either thinking or experiencing death. If you look at the human experience, death will occur frequently and randomly, offering little time for preparation – this is just an inevitable fact. As I work in the area of relationships with people I want to try and change the way others interact with death. Given that none of us know when we will die or face a tragic loss, understanding and navigating death better is likely to enhance our gratitude and improve our relationships while we are alive. The following is my suggestion to peer into this journey.

# Death cafe meetings

Death cafés might sound like they happen in the shadows, yet the reality is they appear all over the world. They have had great success in helping people cope and deal with bereavement since inception thanks to Jon Underwood, a man who died suddenly in 2017. Underwood stated his mission was to redesign and liberate death from "tyrannical secrecy". Deathcafe.com has become a resource where you can explore meetings at cafés worldwide to meet and discuss death and read to find resources around the subject. Initially this might not sound an ideal coffee chat but interestingly, the many I have seen in attendance were not in a state of bereavement. Covid restrictions moved more of these meetings online, but the idea is the same – encouraging a relaxing atmosphere where explorations of death can be discussed. I have partaken in both in-the-room and virtual death cafe discussions, and I have been impressed with the dynamic. There was an opportunity to chat to people worldwide that you may not usually link up with and the format is akin to a networking event but centered on discussing a difficult topic that affects us all. It felt much easier to chat with strangers about hypothetical or real family deaths as opposed to someone I know. Bringing imagery to your mind was something we discussed as a difficult and tough process. An immediate benefit I found leaving meetings was a huge sense of gratitude and the need to tell loved ones how much they were loved. No matter the situation, life keeps on rolling. Whatever we can individually do to embrace this experience will over time become an advantageous life skill. People might highlight the importance of being able to swim but it is easy to avoid the places you might drown. The same cannot be said for death.

# The importance of relationships

You have probably bought this book with the hope of uncovering ways to improve your fitness and nutrition but now find that my key message is not to prioritise these key areas at the expense of relationships. Because that is what I spent most of life doing. Driven for a singular purpose will leave you without high quality social connections. Who really wants that kind of achievement in life?

Some of us enjoy being alone more than others, but interactions still act as the crucial nature defining our species. Achieving and sustaining good health requires a multifaceted approach and must include attention to your relationships. You must not omit this reality from your life. I cannot and will not tell you how to work on something as personal and individual as your relationships, but understand that, just like sleep, physicality, nutrition and cognition, focusing on building and nurturing your relationships will ensure you gain the resilience to survive and prosper in every area of your life that really matters.

Q: If you were about to face your last breath, what messages and guidance would you pass on?

_____

_____

_____

_____

What would you have done differently?

_____

_____

_____

_____

It is extremely hard for many of us to answer these accurately as we are not faced with this being our true reality.

# Relationships case study: Dave Bolton

Dave Bolton served in Iraq, policed the streets of Liverpool as an organised crime detective, and then, tragically, was crushed by an articulated lorry in an accident. Despite being told he wouldn't walk again he went on to win a kickboxing world title. Dave's rollercoaster journey has continued, as he has beaten cancer twice and continues to outlive his terminal six-month brain tumour diagnosis. Dave is now a motivational speaker for companies such as Unilever and is married to my cousin, so I haven't needed to sit in on one of his speeches to appreciate his journey.

Me and Dave became good friends long before his cancer struggle. He traveled much of my journey in MMA and the power of seeing someone you know conquer tough difficulties really does drive you emotionally. The nature of looming death acts as a real catalyst for individual change that needs to occur.

Dave convinced me that the importance of adopting a system to create a necessary structure to keep getting up and actioning good daily habits. None of us know what the future holds; life's adventure will take its turns and then be over. Accepting that now is the best and only moment we have should keep us pushing forward. Dave acts as not only an inspiration but a mentor to my life. Dave currently runs 'Ahead of the Game' foundation (www.aheadofthegamefoundation.com), a CIC working on developing free rehabilitation and support to those suffering from cancer. Who can you look to for inspiration? Further, how can you inspire others with your actions?

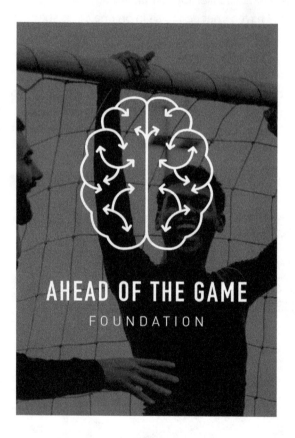

*"Choices are the hinges of destiny."*

Edwin Markham

# With the end in mind

*"A consciousness that everything passes whether good or bad, and the only time that we can experience is this present evanescent moment. This makes hard times slightly easier to bear and good times even more precious."*

Kathryn Moore

The quote above is taken from the book *With the End in Mind* by Kathryn Moore. I am including this in this chapter because we have just discussed death but it could easily be written into the next chapter of balance. Moore relays her experience as a palliative care specialist dealing with death and we can use the lessons passed on from those at the end of their journey. Moore emotionally takes the reader to the determination that *"Life is about balancing your satisfactions with your regrets"*. Too many people wait until they are dying to wish they could have spent their time differently. Regrets are painful and, as Moore explains, they often should have been easy fixes for the people whose minds made them very hard.

A key purpose of KongDay is to help people realise that time is the greatest asset we have. However, if you stop analysing daily you are not accepting this as a true statement, as you are back to just guessing or letting time do its own thing. The dinosaurs roamed the earth for millions of years, yet their time is gone. It is extremely unlikely humans will roam the planet for as long as the dinosaurs did, and of course you certainly won't. Our life expectancy in the UK may have risen to an average of 81 years, contrasted to just 25 years in the 1700s, but we still do not have time to waste. In fact, depending on your age your perception of time will differ. Professor Adrian Bejan tells us that as we age, we process information more slowly, and this is the reason why we feel that time goes faster and faster as we age. I believe it is much simpler than that. Time feels faster as we get older because we reflect on the time we've had and wasted. Once you make the full-time shift to monitoring your scores, time spent is the same regardless of age. Your days should go at exactly the same speed.

# Key Implementations:
## Relationship

> Dedicate set periods for habits that don't benefit you in any way but help others.

> Evaluate and invest a greater percentage of time in your relationships instead of undervaluing them in your life.

> Find new ideas to share and experience.

> Integrate gratitude and journalling daily into your daily life.

> Face up to death.

# My Relationships Score charts for 2020

Relationships - Visual Shades

| | JAN | FEB | MAR | APR | MAY | JUN | JUL | AUG | SEP | OCT | NOV | DEC |
|---|---|---|---|---|---|---|---|---|---|---|---|---|
| 1 | 5 | 4 | 5 | 4 | 4 | 5 | 4 | 5 | 5 | 5 | 4 | 5 |
| 2 | 5 | 4 | 2 | 2 | 5 | 5 | 5 | 4 | 3 | 5 | 4 | 4 |
| 3 | 4 | 2 | 5 | 5 | 4 | 3 | 5 | 4 | 4 | 4 | 5 | 5 |
| 4 | 2 | 3 | 2 | 5 | 3 | 4 | 4 | 4 | 3 | 4 | 5 | 4 |
| 5 | 4 | 5 | 3 | 5 | 4 | 4 | 5 | 5 | 5 | 4 | 5 | 5 |
| 6 | 3 | 5 | 5 | 5 | 4 | 5 | 4 | 4 | 4 | 5 | 5 | 5 |
| 7 | 5 | 3 | 3 | 5 | 4 | 4 | 5 | 2 | 5 | 3 | 5 | 3 |
| 8 | 4 | 2 | 5 | 4 | 3 | 5 | 3 | 5 | 5 | 4 | 5 | 5 |
| 9 | 4 | 1 | 5 | 4 | 3 | 5 | 4 | 4 | 5 | 5 | 4 | 3 |
| 10 | 4 | 2 | 5 | 3 | 3 | 3 | 2 | 3 | 5 | 3 | 5 | 5 |
| 11 | 4 | 4 | 4 | 3 | 4 | 4 | 4 | 5 | 5 | 5 | 3 | 5 |
| 12 | 4 | 5 | 5 | 5 | 4 | 4 | 5 | 4 | 5 | 2 | 5 | 4 |
| 13 | 3 | 3 | 4 | 4 | 3 | 4 | 5 | 5 | 5 | 5 | 5 | 5 |
| 14 | 4 | 2 | 5 | 4 | 5 | 2 | 5 | 5 | 4 | 5 | 5 | 3 |
| 15 | 4 | 4 | 5 | 5 | 4 | 5 | 3 | 5 | 5 | 5 | 5 | 4 |
| 16 | 5 | 5 | 4 | 3 | 5 | 4 | 5 | 4 | 5 | 3 | 4 | 3 |
| 17 | 5 | 2 | 5 | 3 | 5 | 4 | 4 | 3 | 4 | 5 | 5 | 5 |
| 18 | 5 | 4 | 5 | 5 | 5 | 5 | 5 | 5 | 4 | 5 | 3 | 5 |
| 19 | 4 | 2 | 5 | 5 | 4 | 5 | 4 | 5 | 3 | 4 | 4 | 5 |
| 20 | 4 | 4 | 5 | 4 | 4 | 3 | 5 | 5 | 4 | 3 | 5 | 5 |
| 21 | 5 | 3 | 4 | 5 | 4 | 3 | 5 | 5 | 3 | 4 | 5 | 3 |
| 22 | 3 | 4 | 5 | 4 | 5 | 5 | 3 | 5 | 5 | 4 | 4 | 5 |
| 23 | 3 | 4 | 4 | 4 | 3 | 4 | 4 | 4 | 5 | 3 | 4 | 5 |
| 24 | 4 | 2 | 4 | 5 | 4 | 5 | 5 | 4 | 3 | 5 | 4 | 3 |
| 25 | 3 | 5 | 5 | 5 | 4 | 5 | 5 | 4 | 4 | 4 | 3 | 5 |
| 26 | 3 | 3 | 4 | 4 | 5 | 5 | 4 | 4 | 5 | 3 | 3 | 5 |
| 27 | 3 | 4 | 4 | 4 | 3 | 4 | 3 | 4 | 5 | 5 | 4 | 4 |
| 28 | 5 | 3 | 4 | 4 | 4 | 4 | 5 | 5 | 5 | 5 | 5 | 4 |
| 29 | 4 | 5 | 5 | 5 | 5 | 5 | 4 | 4 | 5 | 5 | 4 | 3 |
| 30 | 5 | | 4 | 5 | 5 | 3 | 3 | 3 | 3 | 5 | 4 | 5 |
| 31 | 5 | | 4 | | 4 | | 5 | 4 | | 5 | | 5 |

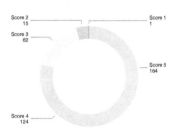

Relationships - Year Score Count

Score 1: 1
Score 2: 15
Score 3: 62
Score 4: 124
Score 5: 164

Relationships Score Counts

| | January | February | March | April | May | June | July | August | September | October | November | December | Total |
|---|---|---|---|---|---|---|---|---|---|---|---|---|---|
| Score 5 | 10 | 6 | 16 | 14 | 10 | 12 | 16 | 12 | 19 | 16 | 15 | 18 | 164 |
| Score 4 | 13 | 9 | 11 | 11 | 14 | 12 | 9 | 15 | 6 | 7 | 11 | 6 | 124 |
| Score 3 | 7 | 6 | 2 | 4 | 7 | 5 | 5 | 3 | 5 | 7 | 4 | 7 | 62 |
| Score 2 | 1 | 7 | 2 | 1 | 0 | 1 | 1 | 1 | 0 | 1 | 0 | 0 | 15 |
| Score 1 | 0 | 1 | 0 | 0 | 0 | 0 | 0 | 0 | 0 | 0 | 0 | 0 | 1 |

KONGDAY: Quantifying your life to success

# 7: BALANCE

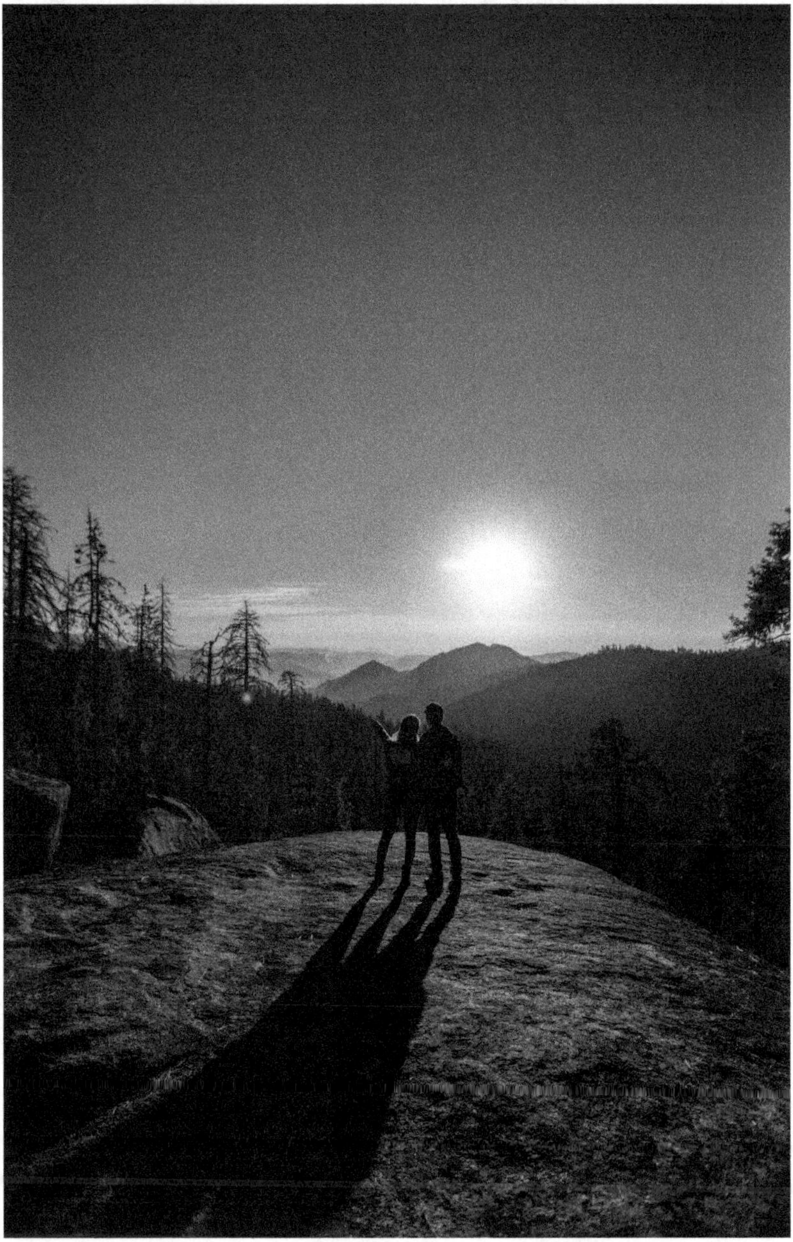

KAZUSHI IS A word the Japanese use in judo when they manage to unbalance an opponent. As a former professional martial artist and now coach, I can underline that balance is the number one fundamental for all martial arts. I have designed the KongDay system of life performance to be founded on the same principle. Without a stable base you have nothing, and the same can be said for our planet. For an ecosystem to survive, only balance and diversity of species make it sustainable. The ebbs and flows of our tides are balanced by the moon and our position is balanced by the sun. You must balance the actions and events of your life to a system that monitors your time spent. How can I be balanced if I spend every day only exercising, studying or working? I must quantify my actions and see how they balance out with each other. You must understand your consistent behaviours.

This chapter on balance purposely comes after the 5 previous chapters, because the real goal is all about how to achieve a balance of the 5:

- Sleep
- Nutrition
- Physicality
- Cognition
- Relationships

*Each one is equally important!*

A similar alignment is seen in the financial investment world, with diversification being the prerequisite to ride tough times. The following image represents balancing your categories as carefully stacked eggs. Without correct balance all the eggs fall and break. Areas will rise and fall and the more you can be spread in the market the less easily you can be wiped out. For KongDay, our most important balance tool is to use quantifiable metrics such as Heart Rate Variability (which we discussed in Physicality) to correctly measure our immune system. This will relay the internal system and you can control the 5 areas above for a complete, effective balance scoring rating.

# Heart Rate Variability (HRV)

We have already highlighted how HRV is a valuable and reliable metric for measuring the state of your nervous system. If you awake with a poor 1/5 HRV score, this reflects a high sympathetic state and a sign that your nervous system is screaming that balance is off. The reason for the 1 reading will need to become part of your investigations to determine the cause affecting your immune response. A 1 in itself is not necessarily bad as it may just be a brief product of previous healthy exertions. But only with recovery or rest can you reestablish a stable immune response.

> *Do not underestimate the importance*
> *of your HRV to guide your life.*

High HRV readings can and will tell you a lot about what makes your relationships, nutrition, physicality and sleep optimal. Take the area of physicality, discussed earlier. With a high HRV reading in the morning we know we should be strenuously pushing fitness and strength levels to give ourselves a top 5 rating in physical activity, because our balance score upon waking has given us the green light. Conversely, waking to a low HRV reading would mean you could still record a 5 for your physicality score but this now requires light walking and recovery therapies instead of the strenuous training session you had planned. Your balance score dictates what a physical session needs to look like, much like a world-class coach would periodically change the structure of an athlete's session based on their fatigue level. If you receive a low score your workday management will need to further change if you want to control your life.

The hardest part about satisfying daily balance is learning to equalize your time between the 5 key KongDay components because deep down, in fact, none of us want to do this. We each enjoy some areas over others and our minds have different priorities. You might currently not value regular exercise or perhaps prioritise sleep but these are all short term, singular goals. To ensure your life and happiness grows in a balanced way you must consistently make sure you dedicate time every day to each KongDay area.

The visual score charts included in this book should be used to help you to achieve this balance. The reason I have included my 2020 data is because it reflects a well-balanced year. I could include data that would support trending upwards and showing clients making the system look great but let's be real. Most of us are probably doing pretty well in one or two of the areas already but that is not enough. When we strive to make parts of our life better, we often look to others for our inspiration, ie the six-pack model that gives us inspiration for our physicality goals. *We often envy a person we know nothing about except for their singular success.* Their six-pack abs to us signifies they are happier than us, with their physique we want. The problem with such a narrow focus is that physicality should only account for 20% of life. Regardless of how well your physical state becomes you remain with a gaping 80% that needs focus. This has been forgotten as all you want is those abs. As I have already mentioned in this book, the professional athlete is a clear example of someone who is probably not physically healthy despite many seeing them as the ideal physicality goal. Even if they were, what does the other 80% of their life look like?

To achieve life greatness, you have to dedicate your time to all areas, with a balanced approach. The athlete sadly does not recognise this due to everyone surrounding them being tasked with winning and nothing else. The athlete's body and life will break down just the same as yours after pursuing such a centric strategy.

Our highest experience of living cannot be created by spending our time always in one or two areas. Sustainability is a good word to use in this context:

*Meeting the needs of the present*
*without compromising the future.*

I have stressed this as the KongDay goal and surprisingly, prison forged an example that the system could always present a way to chase balance, even when limitations are strictly placed upon an individual.

# Case study: Achieving Balance in prison

Initially I was unsure how prisoners could cope and work around implementing my KongDay System, given the restraints and limits to what they were able to do with their time and life behind bars. How well could a prisoner score in nutrition when they couldn't control their food supply? Did they even have sufficient cognitive resources? Relationships? They likely couldn't see the people they wanted to build their key ones with.

Despite all these questions, taking KongDay to prisoners became a challenge and an opportunity to test the system. Within a few months I was reading correspondence from one prisoner who had essentially turned his life around using the system, but not in how I would have expected. After running a diagnostic of his KongDay areas and acknowledging his restrictions, he was left with a strong focus on time to develop his cognitive experience, the classic prisoner reading books if you will.

A plan was made to push cognitive improvements, as the prison system actively encouraged prisoners to take such paths. The difficulty lay in that this was a prisoner who had never read before, and learning this new skill took dedication and perseverance. The prisoner said that before using KongDay, his time inside felt different. The system gave him a clear definition of the exact time he spent reading. Many prisoners can attest to the changing nature of time within prison walls as a famous Dr Seuss quote summarises:

"How did it get late so soon?"

It is not uncommon for prisoners to experience a contradiction of time passing either quicker or slower in its dimension behind bars. Prisoners can suddenly reflect upon decades passed behind bars. In this case, the prisoner was incarcerated for 5 years, almost 2 of those years working with KongDay. This regret of time is just the same as how most of us feel as we get older. Prison just amplifies the waste of time because it becomes easier to question what you have really done in those years. Inside, the prisoner also found a benefit to using the balanced approach:

"I had never really given much thought to analysing how I was spending my time. I had found I had practically stopped training (physical gym work) to spend more of each working day in either my studies or in writing business action plans for when I would be released later. I'm still working on these but spending so much time in one area I thought was me changing my life for the better. At times I built up to a situation of near constant lockdown to read. But I was getting less done in this cognitive area. Lethargy was increasing and I began to realise that an early morning physical program was essential in making sure my cognitive time was more productive. I would be reading books and daydreaming but taking hardly anything in.

I then found the KongDay system empowering because I could see what was happening and attempt to control all the areas. Look, even nutrition was controllable too. I couldn't access foods I wanted but I could choose to use time-restricted eating and learn how to use that to improve my eating behaviours. I got so sick of all the carb-heavy prison meals so I would skip one and keep my carbs lower.

The system is simple, but the beauty of recognising patterns made me realise that without doing this I would have been a mess upon release. I got to see my scores staring at me from my prison wall daily. I could not slack off from yesterday's score or it would start eating me up. I become obsessed with controlling my actions. I believe it has changed the management of my life forever."

I'm not really a fan of including testimonials of my work but it is included here due to the learning it offered me. I naively felt that the individual simply quantifying his time to read more would be the main gain, but all prisons actively encourage this, usually to little success. Why would my approach be any better to help prisoners read than the decades of attempts to change this? Helping to create a life system when the prison was gone was actually the real success I feel KongDay gave. We did however struggle when the person this case study discusses was no longer behind bars. Upon exiting the system after such a long period inside his character was changed but we immediately faced a problem. Reading had become a voracious habit and helped to lead to his chosen route, acquiring a degree from Westminster University but it was achieved because it was easy to sit down to study. There was nothing else to do. On the outside this is still an issue that this person is trying to solve daily.

*Develop your own environment*
*that guarantees balance.*

I'm not sure prison should ever be an ideal environment to focus upon because after all its nature is to act as a deterrent to society. Perhaps we can all try and implement the control of prison scheduling to guarantee set times and quiet periods during our daily routines. This will make balance successful.

# Case Study: Balancing wealth

As an illustration of the diverse nature of the people I have worked with through KongDay, here is a case study about someone also needing balance in their lives, but from a background which is the complete opposite of prison.

One of the earliest clients I worked with was a highly successful telecommunications director who was looking to integrate boxing into her physical goal of losing weight. Interestingly, during our journey of now over 4 years we have since adjusted our focus so that improving relationships is now the core goal. After only a short time of working together the client managed to sell her company and receive significant financial reward for decades of hard work. While life-changing and a moment forever treasured, this was a crucial time to step back and consider the balance in her life and her why.

As the financial ladder is climbed, the addiction to a world which opens up through greater wealth becomes magnetic. Despite her obvious ability to analyse business in a rational, professional and balanced way, there had become many regrets over missing time with her family while work took priority.

By tapping into her professional skills but re-prioritising them, we created quantifiable, daily objectives in a wider range of areas of her life. Now the focus became to choose and prioritise family time alongside continuing to work on exercise and movement too. After all, the sole reason for all the hard work and wealth creation had been legacy and security for her children and beyond to theirs. Health had become a focus too because the stress and nature of high-powered business had meant weight had piled on.

In following this new approach daily, the client has successfully found balance in her life – namely more quality relationship time and not at the expense of working on physical goals. She now sits at her lowest and leanest physical measurements since adulthood.

The interesting lesson I have found from this is that wealth, unless put into perspective and managed as part of a regime of balance and priorities, is not a fix in itself. Money, just like any area, can create and compound a situation to be more positive or more negative. Only when we handle the dynamic will it turn to our advantage. It is easy to sit from afar and view those wealthier than ourselves as having an easier time managing the processes of life but in fact, it can be quite the reverse. With increased access and opportunities, structure becomes more important as the danger of being able to do more takes a person further away from repeating the same daily behaviours.

## Case Study: Living the dream

My third example of someone finding balance through KongDay, is someone who finally felt liberated in their thinking to pursue their dream.

A marketing director I began working with came to me to explore how he could balance his life, as he felt his work, which was running his own company, had left him viewing years passing with nothing but monetary and business gain. An all-too familiar problem for many people. The client did not have any specific goals but wanted to explore the system to see how it might help him figure out balancing his life.

Fast forward 9 months and he has sold his company and is now chasing a long-held desire to join the military. Despite being right at the cut-off age for full-time recruitment he is close to passing the full selection process. At first this was a journey that meant he would enter the reserves and serve for a small number of days during a calendar year. The client had undergone a hip operation previously which would normally rule out passing a medical exam. By targeted physical training we worked with my old university sports science centre and a respected surgeon to produce evidence that mobility and strength of the joint is as robust as that of any other entrant.

Regardless of the final outcome, he now feels he has a system which, in his own words, has given him a way to finally satisfy his soul. As I learnt from my time as a mixed martial artist the journey is the treasure, not results or events. For me, no amount of money can ever buy the unique experience I was lucky enough to experience and use to form my character. Unless we find ways to expand our experience, we can feel that our job and life is a drain. We can become envious of the low-waged worker who seems to have free time and a carefree approach to life. Once we become engaged in the system of regular working hours, we can lose much of the spirit we have as children.

Writing about this case study example of someone breaking free to pursue a long-held dream reminded me of one of the saddest conversations I have ever had with my son, after he just turned 5. It was late and he couldn't sleep, and we lay chatting in his room. He asked me why adults have to go to work, to which I replied they don't have to but often choose to so that the children do not have to work and can spend their time having as much fun as possible. Hoping this might score me some dad points, the reply was not what I enjoyed hearing. He replied that maybe I could decide to have more fun instead of working so much. Despite me creating a life that placed regular importance on all the areas of KongDay, my own son's vision was one of a dad that worked too much. This was another reminder to not simply accept my own scores but include the perspective of others, in this case someone close to me, in how I should be scoring my areas for improvement. I have since tried to increase the time of laughter and play and be more childlike, even when he is not around!

# A system for everyone

I believe the KongDay system should work regardless of the environment. What about for children at school? Most parents use a stickered chart for their children to use to complete tasks and gain rewards. You might encourage them to tidy their room or to be kind, but wouldn't these charts be better served having them focus on the five categories described here?

*Encouraging children to strive every day to work on their relationships, physicality, nutrition, cognition and sleep are a better use of time and energy for everyone.*

How about people now living in retirement that might have more time due to no longer working full time? How are they currently adopting the daily routine of monitoring sleep, physicality, cognition, nutrition and relationships? *At what age are none of these important?* At what age would any person not benefit by taking charge of these areas themselves over waiting for others to do it for them?

## Consider others

An area of balance you should begin to look at is your consideration of others. We have already discussed your immediate circle of others, to which you listed your circle of 5, but what about the others beyond that? A key component of balance is to think beyond your own needs and those of your immediate circle. As a challenging thought, why not see if you can aim at achieving a target of giving 5% of your income to charity? Or to devoting (at least) 5% of your time each week to helping others, through volunteering or some charitable work. At some point in our lives we will need compassion shown to us and hope that others will help.

Adding this dimension of others to your balance category helps to satisfy our need for finding a purpose and meaning in life. If we could all just do a little bit more then we could truly eradicate global poverty but also many challenges and issues closer to home. Having a part of your KongDay focused on what you do for others will go a long way to creating an optimal future and existence for us all.

## The power of stoicism

I will now describe why you should consider applying the ancient practice of stoicism to your life. The most famous of the stoics would be Seneca, Epictetus, Marcus Aurelius or to a lesser extent the stoic founder, Zeno of Citium. During their time stoicism was the religion of the time (before Christianity came to town) and self-control was central to how you managed to live. The world used to be inherent with many more dangers and tragedies. Marcus Aurelius by the year 166 had lost 9 of his children. His meditations are a stoic text about how he dealt with much of this grief. Can you imagine losing 9 children?

The stoicism reemergence is due to how it successfully helps users with an ability to suffer less and control reactions to the events of life. Without this ability the Greeks alluded it is impossible to achieve *eudaimonia* (happiness). We are back again to this idea that an **individual's ability to withstand suffering without complaint is essential**. This is simply because we are all going to suffer in life. We will become depressed and face problems, some much more than others because a person's situation is a pure chance correlation. Much like I implore you to embrace and face the reality of death, many schools today might benefit from teaching and applying stoic principles as opposed to their current religious syllabus. A great introduction to the value of stoicism is the book *Zen Shorts* by John Muth. Some may claim it is aimed at children, but the book reflects Japanese culture mixed with stoic responses to deliver powerful and thought-provoking messages. The word 'maybe' is repeated constantly throughout the story as the justification for why something has happened. Think about how a *'maybe'* for the reason as to why something has happened leaves any scenario as the possible reason. Nothing can be truly blamed or cited so emotion and anger is omitted.

## Stop multitasking!

For a long time, I became obsessed with overproduction. The urge to constantly increase the efficiency of my time was, I thought, a way to have more time for other actions. Many people begin the system with the same want. However, this is not using time optimally. I used to create an illusion of finding more time by methods such as listening to audiobooks while driving. An 8hr book on Audible would only take me 4 hours due to training my ear to listen comfortably at 2x speed. Did this really make any difference to the time saved? *Maybe!*

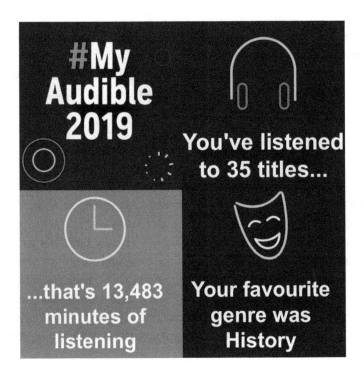

The problem I found with this productivity obsession was that it constantly promoted multitasking. I couldn't eat my breakfast without reading, or lift weights without making phone calls, because I believed I was getting more done in the same time window. However, real deep mindful states are only achieved when you uni-task, with your focus on just one area.

I encourage you to use the system but focus on achieving a mindful state. You want to spend your brief time on the planet focused and relaxed on what you are doing at that moment. People practise mindfulness to look for this, but only seem to gain the benefits in those short meditative periods. Manage your life so you enjoy the time you have. Why rush? I slowed myself down by telling myself that I was just rushing to the grave. The faster I got tasks done the faster I was one step closer to death.

*A true master doesn't need*
*mindfulness, as life is mindful.*

Slow time down by slowing your rush. If you're reading a book, read it. *Airplane mode your life.* Know that when it is time to work on your relationships, you are actually working on your relationships, not just out for a coffee with your spouse while still checking your phone or answering business calls.

*Start today the art of uni-tasking.*

See how time feels when you absorb yourself in the moment. I have found this actually creates a perception of more time. Often, walking or driving somewhere I will focus on a bend and notice how long it actually takes me to reach the bend. Sometimes my mind slows down the experience so much I feel like the bend is almost not real. Despite this I do accept that time is the same and we all experience 525,600 minutes per year. No matter our location, situation or wealth, the clock is fixed. What better way of living than every day enjoying relationships, good nutritious food, sleeping well, exercising and stimulating your brain?

*How you choose to break down your day of 1440 minutes into balancing 5 essential areas is entirely up to you.*

The important thing is to start because momentum causes flow. Ensure your daily stream runs smoothly so your flow turns into a massive tidal momentum given time and patience. No one else is going to come along and help you – if anything they will pull water out of your stream for their own momentum.

# Use the power of music

An auxiliary intervention I have included in my own balance routine is the practice of listening to one song with my eyes closed to invoke powerful emotions. This doesn't have to be one that holds strong ties to you, but it helps for me. Given I had around 100 competitive fights I have 100 walkout tracks that remind me of past days in an instant. It is quite easy for me to simply play a song with my eyes closed and transport myself back to the same physical feeling of tingly sensations and unknown fear. It also acts as a way to switch off from certain distractions which may have entered my head.

I have concluded that leaving part of my day to include 3-4 mins to sit or dance in a private space and let my body be nourished by music just makes me feel good. The importance for me here is that the music is deeply mindful. I am never distracted by another person or a phone in this time. I do not allow my experience to be interrupted. Any event in life can wait those 3-4 minutes because what could I really do anyway?

This ritual of music is also used by many fighters pre-fight to psych themselves up backstage. Close your eyes and listen to music with your closed eyes. Whatever your reason, music is a proven way to boost mood, and your mood affects balance, and you might benefit from immersive, focused periods.

# Key Implementations:
## Balance

> Organise a routine that helps you to live a balanced day, every day.

> Log and use your Heart Rate Variability daily to balance your life's inputs to increase output capacity.

> Move away from multitasking, as it's counterproductive!

> Experiment with these balance-enhancing techniques: carve out time/ resources for charity + helping others; adopt stoicism; harness the mindful use of music.

> Life is unpredictable, so don't stress about short term imbalances. They are a healthy effect of life. Focus on long-term management that means they do not become systemic stress.

# My Balance Score charts for 2020

Balance - Visual Shades

|     | JAN | FEB | MAR | APR | MAY | JUN | JUL | AUG | SEP | OCT | NOV | DEC |
|-----|-----|-----|-----|-----|-----|-----|-----|-----|-----|-----|-----|-----|
| 1   | 2 | 3 | 3 | 3 | 4 | 4 | 5 | 4 | 5 | 5 | 3 | 3 |
| 2   | 3 | 3 | 2 | 3 | 5 | 4 | 4 | 1 | 5 | 4 | 3 | 4 |
| 3   | 2 | 3 | 4 | 4 | 4 | 2 | 5 | 5 | 5 | 5 | 5 | 4 |
| 4   | 3 | 3 | 3 | 4 | 5 | 3 | 4 | 5 | 5 | 5 | 5 | 5 |
| 5   | 3 | 3 | 3 | 4 | 4 | 4 | 4 | 4 | 4 | 5 | 5 | 2 |
| 6   | 3 | 3 | 3 | 2 | 4 | 4 | 4 | 4 | 2 | 5 | 4 | 5 |
| 7   | 4 | 3 | 3 | 4 | 4 | 4 | 3 | 2 | 4 | 3 | 5 | 4 |
| 8   | 2 | 3 | 2 | 2 | 5 | 3 | 3 | 4 | 4 | 4 | 5 | 5 |
| 9   | 4 | 1 | 4 | 4 | 2 | 5 | 2 | 5 | 5 | 4 | 2 | 5 |
| 10  | 4 | 2 | 4 | 4 | 2 | 4 | 5 | 5 | 5 | 5 | 5 | 4 |
| 11  | 4 | 3 | 3 | 2 | 4 | 4 | 4 | 5 | 2 | 5 | 5 | 4 |
| 12  | 4 | 3 | 3 | 4 | 2 | 3 | 4 | 4 | 2 | 3 | 3 | 4 |
| 13  | 3 | 2 | 4 | 3 | 4 | 3 | 4 | 4 | 4 | 3 | 3 | 4 |
| 14  | 3 | 2 | 2 | 3 | 4 | 4 | 4 | 5 | 5 | 5 | 4 | 5 |
| 15  | 3 | 3 | 3 | 4 | 3 | 4 | 3 | 2 | 4 | 4 | 4 | 5 |
| 16  | 4 | 3 | 3 | 4 | 3 | 4 | 3 | 5 | 3 | 5 | 4 | 4 |
| 17  | 3 | 2 | 3 | 3 | 5 | 4 | 3 | 5 | 5 | 3 | 2 | 4 |
| 18  | 3 | 3 | 3 | 4 | 5 | 4 | 3 | 4 | 4 | 4 | 5 | 5 |
| 19  | 4 | 4 | 3 | 5 | 4 | 3 | 2 | 5 | 4 | 5 | 3 | 5 |
| 20  | 3 | 1 | 3 | 3 | 4 | 3 | 5 | 5 | 4 | 5 | 3 | 5 |
| 21  | 2 | 2 | 2 | 4 | 3 | 4 | 4 | 4 | 3 | 5 | 3 | 2 |
| 22  | 3 | 2 | 3 | 3 | 4 | 2 | 5 | 4 | 4 | 5 | 4 | 4 |
| 23  | 3 | 3 | 4 | 3 | 4 | 4 | 4 | 4 | 5 | 5 | 4 | 4 |
| 24  | 4 | 3 | 4 | 3 | 2 | 4 | 5 | 2 | 2 | 4 | 3 | 3 |
| 25  | 3 | 4 | 3 | 5 | 3 | 4 | 3 | 5 | 4 | 3 | 4 | 3 |
| 26  | 3 | 3 | 3 | 2 | 3 | 4 | 3 | 4 | 3 | 4 | 4 | 3 |
| 27  | 3 | 3 | 3 | 4 | 2 | 4 | 4 | 4 | 4 | 5 | 5 | 2 |
| 28  | 3 | 3 | 3 | 5 | 4 | 4 | 5 | 4 | 5 | 4 | 4 | 5 |
| 29  | 3 | 3 | 4 | 2 | 3 | 4 | 3 | 5 | 4 | 4 | 4 | 5 |
| 30  | 2 |   | 2 | 3 | 2 | 4 | 5 | 5 | 4 | 4 | 4 | 5 |
| 31  | 4 |   | 4 |   | 4 |   | 4 | 5 |   | 5 |   | 3 |

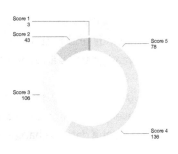

Balance - Year Score Count

- Score 1: 3
- Score 2: 43
- Score 3: 106
- Score 4: 136
- Score 5: 78

Sleep Score Counts

|         | January | February | March | April | May | June | July | August | September | October | November | December | Total |
|---------|---------|----------|-------|-------|-----|------|------|--------|-----------|---------|----------|----------|-------|
| Score 5 | 0 | 0 | 0 | 3 | 5 | 1 | 7 | 14 | 11 | 16 | 9 | 12 | 78 |
| Score 4 | 9 | 2 | 8 | 12 | 14 | 21 | 13 | 13 | 12 | 10 | 11 | 11 | 136 |
| Score 3 | 17 | 19 | 18 | 10 | 6 | 6 | 9 | 0 | 3 | 5 | 8 | 5 | 106 |
| Score 2 | 5 | 6 | 5 | 0 | 0 | 2 | 2 | 0 | 4 | 0 | 0 | 0 | 10 |
| Score 1 | 0 | 2 | 0 | 0 | 0 | 0 | 0 | 1 | 0 | 0 | 0 | 0 | 3 |

Below is a simplified bullet point checklist to use for creating optimal balance.

# Measure and track your journey to achieving balance

- **COLLECT AS MUCH DATA AS POSSIBLE:** Please note that what you may come across as an optimal diet or lifestyle described will never be completely transferable to you.

- **SCORES CREATE VISUAL GRAPHS AND FEEDBACK:** Track key periods and patterns in your behaviour and actions. See the included yearly data as an example.

- **QUANTIFY YOUR HABITS:** Monitoring apps now allow you to view your user history and time spent on devices in daily or weekly time periods. Use the data to change your time.

- **FIND PATTERNS:** Perhaps you always boost your relationship score on Sunday but otherwise perform poorly in this area weekly. Once you find patterns you can begin interventions to make accurate positive changes.

- **BE IN SCHOOL:** The learning journey sadly finishes for many after school, unless you take on a mentor or continue to cultivate an interest in a subject. Develop a mindset which always wants to keep learning.

# 8: SCORING YOUR JOURNEY

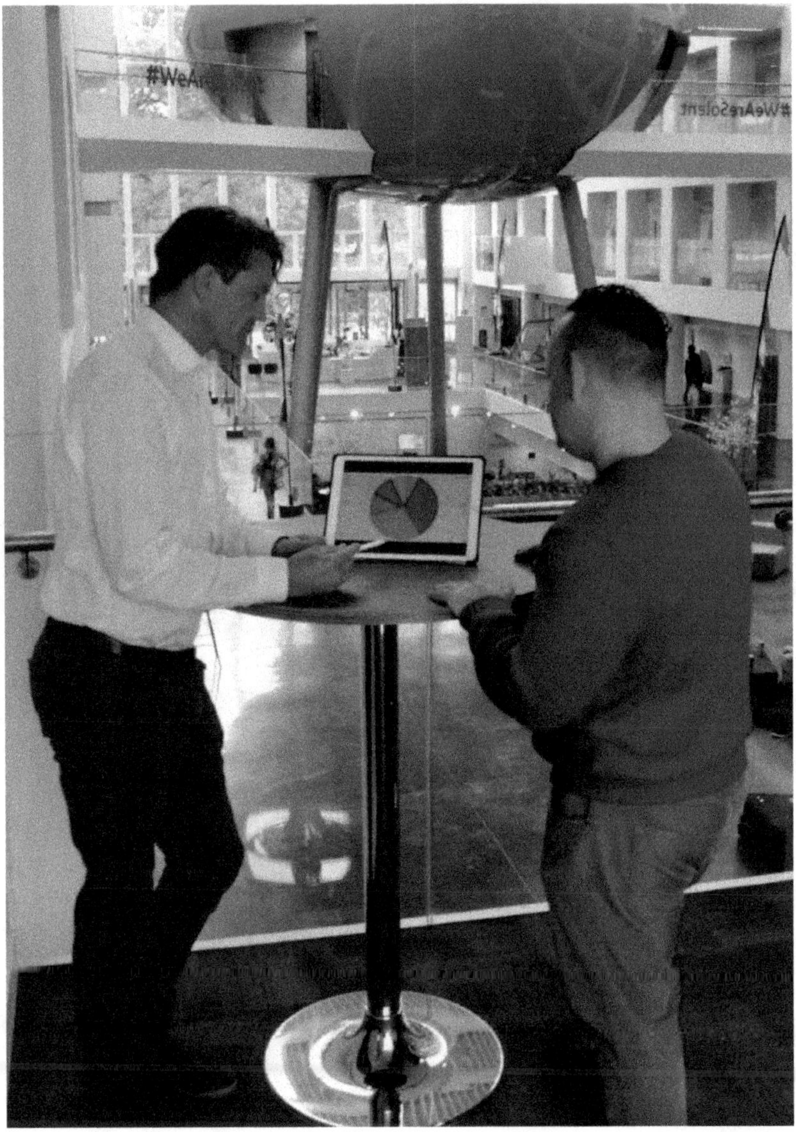

THE KEY TO success in using the KongDay system is to adopt the tools correctly. The more rigorous you can measure and score your 6 categories, the better you analyse your time and life.

Now you have a firm grasp of each of the 6 KongDay categories, I need to help you establish the best way to score each category both accurately and regularly.

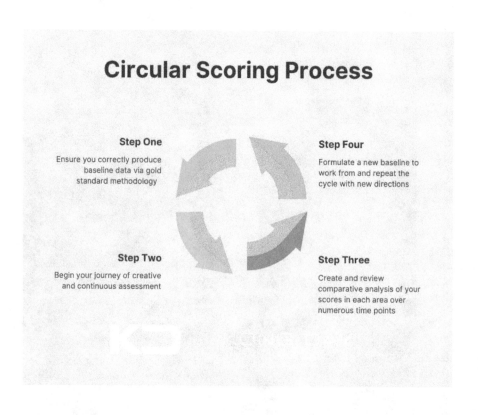

# Circular Scoring Process

**Step One**

Ensure you correctly produce baseline data via gold standard methodology

**Step Four**

Formulate a new baseline to work from and repeat the cycle with new directions

**Step Two**

Begin your journey of creative and continuous assessment

**Step Three**

Create and review comparative analysis of your scores in each area over numerous time points

STEP ONE is producing your baseline score (where you are now). For example, when monitoring physical performance, a gold standard data evaluation could include dexa scans, which relay the current most scientifically accurate measurements of body fat, bone density and visceral fat stores. Further in *Physicality*, you can assess your heart rate, your unique body history (surgeries, limitations etc) and a host of strength and cardiovascular (vo2 Max) tests to keep accumulating data.

**STEP TWO** is you starting your journey and progress over time (without quantifying this in numbers as you have yet to analyse and critique the action).

**STEP THREE** is to plot the scores you have made each day since your baseline data and evaluate how time has revealed your actions.

**STEP FOUR** is to set your new baseline scores and begin the cycle again.

*The above process is designed to create a constant improvement cycle. Areas will rise and fall but you will strive to keep your average scores trending upward and deal with falls and actions.*

Now, the scientists amongst you will be screaming that a self-evaluation cannot be reliable, but we will try as much as possible to do the best we can. By focusing on the quality of the data, not the quantity, you can add some non-emotive, numerical input to level up your experience and behaviour.

*Resist the temptation to compare your
scores with those of others — just look at your
data and your progress, no one else's.*

In the future, I expect data tracking and collection methods to advance which will make your system even more scientific in its scoring. From sleeping to physicality, it's likely technology will produce better tools we can use to improve the accuracy of our scores.

# Introduction to KongDay scoring guidelines

## Example: Physicality

You have a goal to lose weight as you have increased to a BMI measurement that classifies you as obese. You set yourself the simple target of 2000 calories per day as your maximum consumption allowance, which you will balance against 1000 calories per day to be expended in exercise. If you do not exercise on a certain day, then your energy in would be adapted because there is no longer 1000 calories going out of your system. With this approach you figure in the long term you can bring your weight down to a healthy BMI rating. You make this your only goal for your physicality scoring and decide it will be simple to score yourself a 1 when you expend under 200 calories in your workouts. You keep this theme going up in increments of 200 to mean a 5 score is when you hit your 1000 calorie daily expenditure goal. This now becomes your scoring system.

You can ultimately use and design your own scoring to be as complex or as easy as you like. The example above means you have created a clear quantifiable method to show accountability for how you are sticking to your goal. You should then additionally produce your own charts of performance from this data and visually see your scores. This will motivate you and keep you witnessing daily and longer-term results. Later, you might add other physicality scoring guidelines that increase the complexity of your scoring methods. Either way you can quickly access snapshot data and contrast time periods to update future physicality goals. Your ultimate goal in this example is to lose weight, so this should be tracked too, in parallel with the monitoring of calorie intake and levels of physical activity. Keep returning to your data charts and your journalling and devise new physical programming, just like an elite coach.

# Sustaining motivation

Clients are often fearful that once they start hitting higher scores the system will become boring because the target has been reached. You might be on a streak and at the point of near 30/30 KongDay daily scores consistently. You could think that the system is complete. You did it. The perfect day, not much to improve upon from there, but of course there is always a next step. Look at elite sport or business. Now you want to extend this streak and see how you might take your performance to new levels. You will soon find that the enjoyment and pleasure that comes from 30/30 scoring days means you will want more! Rest assured, I haven't seen many 30 KongDay scores anyway! It is very hard to smash everything out of the park in the 5 key areas of life. Life has a way of throwing challenges that will do their best to hammer down your KongDay score. The subjective nature of self-scoring and progression means you may become tougher in your scoring assessment further advancing your progress.

# KongDay scoring guidelines

Here are my notes to help you to create a scoring system for each category which will help you to track these accurately. You may wish to remember the earlier acronym to remember the categories, if journalling by hand. :

**S**leep
**R**elationships
**B**alance
**P**hysicality
**N**utrition
**C**ognition

The best time to perform this rating is around one hour after waking. Do not reach immediately for your phone upon waking to register your sleep score. Leave yourself ample time to rise and move before reflecting on the quality of your sleep last night. Key aspects to factor will be length of time asleep and disturbances experienced during that time. If pairing with a sleep monitoring tool, consider the data from it to complete your sleep score.

## Scoring your sleep 1-5

Note: If you have experienced higher levels of physical muscular exhaustion or stress then add 1 hour to the time you need asleep.

1: A total of less than 3 hours of sleep; insomnia and anxiety throughout most of your sleep.
2: 3-5 hours' sleep
3: 5-6 hours' sleep
4: 6-7 hours' sleep
5: 8+ hours' sleep, no disturbances. Optimal sleep environment (comfort of bed and blackout space)

# Nutrition

Arguably the most difficult category to score for your KongDay rating. Too frequently the prescription of correct and definitive ways to eat is wrong. It is not necessarily important what type of eating protocol you follow; the KongDay rating is concerned about your adherence to sticking to your plan. Regardless of strategy you should be looking for whole foods and a high micronutrient profile regardless of your macro split. If pairing with a food logging tool, consider scoring according to how close you hit your daily goal of calories/macros etc. It is also worth considering HRV to try and find food sources that affect your nervous system the most. The key area we find our clients omit in nutrition scoring is beverages. For every alcoholic drink outside of the healthy odd glass of wine (per blue zones guidance) minus a 1 rating from whatever score you have. Also consider the role of soft drinks and other beverages that would change your score as these too are not optimal.

## Scoring your daily nutrition 1-5

1: Poor choices and low levels of energy with little to no micronutrient or energy dense foods. You are likely to feel sluggish after eating in this rating area. If you have set a goal to eliminate/change food/nutrition choices but skipped them today, consider awarding yourself a 1 rating!

2: You slipped off the wagon a few times today but did satisfy a basic requirement of macronutrient profile to give you energy. If you are fasting and felt great during this period, ignore the previous rating and place yourself towards the top of the ratings for nutrition.

3: Steady progression towards your peak nutrition. You likely ate well across a varied and healthy protocol. Consider a 3 rating if you skipped meals or chose poor/rushed eating periods outside of fasting.

4: Long-term eating at a 4 rating is fantastic for long-term health and is likely the most sustainable way to achieve results. You only missed a 5-rating due to a minor slip in food choice or timing/sticking to your nutrition goals.

5: The balance of micro/macro is considered to be perfect in this rating. Energy levels were through the roof during your working day and exercise sessions. You have tried many ways to eat, and this current methodology is giving you far greater tangible good feedback than other methods previously employed.

# Physicality

Do not think of scoring fitness as purely 1-5 reflecting how hard you worked in your daily exercise. An extremely grueling physical or heavy strength session for example may not always reflect a 5 score. This does not mean you should omit them to achieve a regular 5 score, but it is important to consider the role the session plays in your development of healthy movements rather than view it as a single daily score. Also, rather than just considering calories burned or HR zones, consider movement and flexibility as another way to score a high rating.

## Scoring your physicality 1-5

1: You did nothing to reflect movement quality or improvements in your fitness/exercise goals.
2: Small or little work was done but better than a 1 score.
3: Solid progress was made to moving well today and getting your heart rate (HR) above a baseline level of purely functional life.
4: A perfect balance of raising your HR and working on improving specific exercise goals. You may have pushed too hard for improvements for the future so that prevents you from achieving a 5 score but that doesn't make this worse than a 5 rating necessarily.
5: You met all of your fitness goals and satisfied workout times that you have set, or new challenges were achieved.

# Cognition

The scoring of cognition is focused on working on ways you stimulate your mind. Too often, fitness and health/lifestyle trackers are focused on physical metrics rather than the development of cognitive functions. For this area you should consider learning new skills and rewarding yourself accordingly. Monitor time spent developing new skills such as learning a language or playing a musical instrument. Reading and a host of other areas are included in this category. Also consider the effect stress and work may play on bringing this score down regardless of meeting such learning/improvements objectives.

## Scoring your cognition 1-5

1: No time was given to any area you would consider a cognitive advancement.
2: Little time was dedicated to giving your mind a workout.
3: You managed to dedicate up to 30 mins towards new skills/learning.
4: 30 mins-2 hours was dedicated towards improving your cognitive abilities.
5: 2hrs+ was achieved and unrushed in this area of mental self-improvement.

# Relationships

The pinnacle of living a happy life. Clearly scoring a 5 across the previous four categories is paramount but this would not equate to a positive result if your relationship score was a 1 rating. Therefore, this category you review at the end of the day should have huge focus. To consider how you rate this section you might want to make ratings during the day and adjust accordingly as you encounter different emotions during the day.

KongDay urges you to consider mindfulness app integration such as Headspace and using gratitude reflection in deciding your score for the day. For many of our clients this section is also influenced by loved ones. A bad day for your child will likely alter your rating of daily happiness, so how these affect you and your reactions to them should be reflected in your score. Due to the uncontrollable nature of other people, it is harder to control this area as much as others in the KongDay system. However, a look toward stoicism and fair reflection can improve the way in which you react to events and affect your scoring here.

## Scoring your relationships 1-5

1: Scoring a 1 here means your day and elements of your life couldn't have gone much worse. As with other categories, prolonged scoring in a 1 area should trigger an intervention into significant life changes.

2: Signifies an attempt to foster positivity and gratitude but situations/ stressors in your day heavily impacted your ability to smile throughout the day.

3: Simply not unhappy but likewise not ending the day with a happy review and outlook. Likely you didn't take time to sit and reflect to enjoy the present enough to be in the higher ratings. Also, while you cannot be responsible for others' feelings, if you are causing negative emotions during communication with others, this will hinder you scoring any higher than this. Happiness is internal but should not come at the expense of others.

4: Great work towards creating a great atmosphere for all those people that interact with you during the day, either in person or digitally.

5: No explanation needed – you're just happy and grateful for this day. What a day!

# Balance

Make an analysis on the balance within your five categories. If you scored 3 across all the categories that is more balanced than a 5 in some and 1s in the others. Pair this balance evaluation to your HRV and readiness data. Your balance should include how you feel and what your immune system relays.

## Scoring your balance 1-5

1: Nervous system is in a high sympathetic state and you failed to dedicate time to other categories of KongDay.

2: Some sympathetic response and only managing to cover some of the areas of KongDay.

3: Consistent split between time in all categories and average readiness.

4: Immune system reflects good parasympathetic scoring and most categories had over 5% of daily time dedicated to improvement.

5: You feel amazing! Your readiness is up at peak scores and you smashed dedication to all of the KongDay categories. A true KongDay!

| | JAN | FEB | MAR | APR | MAY | JUN | JUL | AUG | SEP | OCT | NOV | DEC |
|---|---|---|---|---|---|---|---|---|---|---|---|---|
| 1 | 18 | 19 | 22 | 20 | 26 | 22 | 23 | 18 | 24 | 23 | 23 | 20 |
| 2 | 20 | 21 | 17 | 22 | 24 | 17 | 24 | 13 | 22 | 25 | 21 | 24 |
| 3 | 16 | 17 | 22 | 22 | 25 | 17 | 26 | 24 | 21 | 25 | 24 | 25 |
| 4 | 17 | 21 | 17 | 21 | 23 | 22 | 20 | 23 | 20 | 25 | 22 | 22 |
| 5 | 22 | 20 | 18 | 24 | 20 | 21 | 24 | 21 | 23 | 23 | 24 | 21 |
| 6 | 19 | 22 | 19 | 17 | 20 | 25 | 23 | 19 | 13 | 25 | 22 | 24 |
| 7 | 23 | 20 | 19 | 23 | 19 | 23 | 19 | 16 | 21 | 19 | 24 | 22 |
| 8 | 20 | 19 | 19 | 16 | 24 | 25 | 21 | 19 | 24 | 22 | 23 | 24 |
| 9 | 25 | 13 | 25 | 23 | 17 | 25 | 19 | 27 | 26 | 18 | 20 | 25 |
| 10 | 25 | 16 | 24 | 23 | 17 | 22 | 22 | 25 | 27 | 19 | 24 | 25 |
| 11 | 22 | 20 | 19 | 19 | 21 | 21 | 17 | 23 | 16 | 26 | 26 | 24 |
| 12 | 24 | 18 | 18 | 26 | 21 | 19 | 21 | 22 | 16 | 18 | 23 | 22 |
| 13 | 22 | 20 | 22 | 22 | 22 | 20 | 21 | 22 | 25 | 21 | 25 | 24 |
| 14 | 22 | 16 | 18 | 22 | 23 | 18 | 19 | 25 | 26 | 26 | 22 | 25 |
| 15 | 21 | 19 | 21 | 24 | 21 | 24 | 20 | 23 | 23 | 24 | 22 | 22 |
| 16 | 26 | 18 | 18 | 23 | 21 | 24 | 23 | 24 | 25 | 18 | 24 | 21 |
| 17 | 20 | 17 | 18 | 21 | 23 | 25 | 22 | 26 | 26 | 17 | 19 | 20 |
| 18 | 18 | 18 | 21 | 26 | 28 | 24 | 21 | 22 | 19 | 26 | 26 | 20 |
| 19 | 24 | 23 | 20 | 25 | 19 | 23 | 22 | 21 | 23 | 24 | 24 | 26 |
| 20 | 19 | 16 | 20 | 21 | 22 | 18 | 27 | 22 | 23 | 24 | 25 | 25 |
| 21 | 17 | 17 | 19 | 26 | 18 | 24 | 26 | 24 | 18 | 25 | 19 | 21 |
| 22 | 22 | 15 | 19 | 23 | 23 | 21 | 24 | 23 | 23 | 23 | 22 | 23 |
| 23 | 20 | 18 | 20 | 24 | 20 | 21 | 21 | 19 | 22 | 21 | 24 | 21 |
| 24 | 22 | 16 | 23 | 23 | 20 | 22 | 25 | 16 | 17 | 24 | 22 | 17 |
| 25 | 19 | 23 | 23 | 26 | 22 | 24 | 18 | 24 | 18 | 23 | 24 | 20 |
| 26 | 21 | 18 | 21 | 18 | 20 | 20 | 15 | 23 | 25 | 25 | 23 | 20 |
| 27 | 20 | 19 | 21 | 23 | 21 | 22 | 24 | 22 | 25 | 24 | 24 | 22 |
| 28 | 21 | 17 | 19 | 24 | 21 | 21 | 21 | 24 | 25 | 21 | 19 | 25 |
| 29 | 17 | 22 | 23 | 22 | 17 | 22 | 22 | 21 | 28 | 22 | 20 | 23 |
| 30 | 18 | | 20 | 23 | 20 | 18 | 22 | 20 | 23 | 23 | 25 | 25 |
| 31 | 23 | | 23 | | 27 | | 21 | 24 | | 23 | | 21 |

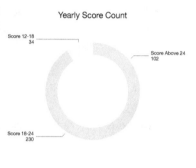

### Yearly Score Count

Score 12-18
34

Score Above 24
102

Score 18-24
230

| | January | February | March | April | May | June | July | August | September | October | November | December | Total |
|---|---|---|---|---|---|---|---|---|---|---|---|---|---|
| Score Above 24 | 5 | 0 | 2 | 9 | 6 | 9 | 8 | 10 | 12 | 14 | 14 | 13 | 102 |
| Score 18-24 | 22 | 19 | 27 | 19 | 22 | 19 | 21 | 18 | 14 | 16 | 16 | 17 | 230 |
| Score 12-18 | 4 | 10 | 2 | 2 | 3 | 2 | 2 | 3 | 4 | 1 | 0 | 1 | 34 |
| Score 6-12 | 0 | 0 | 0 | 0 | 0 | 0 | 0 | 0 | 0 | 0 | 0 | 0 | 0 |
| Score Below 6 | 0 | 0 | 0 | 0 | 0 | 0 | 0 | 0 | 0 | 0 | 0 | 0 | 0 |

# Quantifying a successful day

I want to break down what a successful day might look like in quantifiable time segments to know how to structure our time. Using my personalised template, you can tweak ideal hours into percentages, to work towards hitting daily targets of compliance. For me, I have recently settled on a strong focus toward cognitive improvements, sleep and relationship quality over physicality and nutrition, but this is unique to my current situation. Adapt as required for you and your priorities.

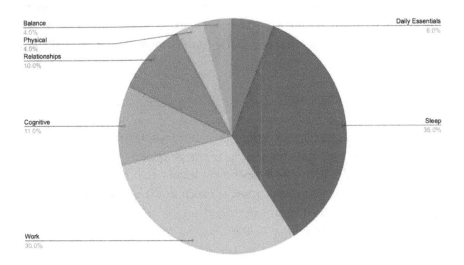

## Sleep: 35% daily

This is 8hrs in bed per night. Just over 8hrs equates to 35% of our 24hr day. Based on 4 months prior sleep tracking I have found, as discussed, that ideally, I am in bed by 10 for better quality. Regardless, if I am due to wake up at 6.30am I will need to be in bed by 10.15pm to have any shot at an 8hr sleep time.

We now have 75% to allocate to 4 remaining categories. For me this might be best optimised as follows:

## Physicality: 4% daily

This works out at 1 hour per day, and for me, I have found one hour easily sufficient as I am not focused on long heart rate training sessions. Given I spent pretty much most of the last 25 years as a professional athlete I believe I also have an extensive base of training to make it much easier to get my physicality goals done in an hour. Also, factor in that as a mixed martial arts coach a lot of my working time is physical. I have described this back in my step count in the Physicality chapter.

My current program is usually 20-30 mins of heavy strength and explosive work, with the remaining being mobility and flexibility training due to already and genetically having a high Vo2 max. 2-3 times monthly I will swap the strength for endurance and spend the full 1-1.2 hours working on my heart rate zones. Then I will omit the strength training goal and switch instead for a heart rate day.

## Nutrition: 0% daily

Given my wife cooks fantastic meals daily for our family I only need to set aside a small amount of time daily for making or prepping food that I will consume, such as granola. I also occasionally spend any extra free time (later mentioned in Balance) studying hours of a masterclass such as the previously mentioned Gordon Ramsay's masterclass online but did not feel the need to block a daily specific time of focus for nutrition in this example.

## Cognition: 11% daily

I am currently breaking this down as follows into a period of 2.5 hrs per day.

Currently this involves 30 mins of Spanish via an app and 10 mins of Spanish news on YouTube. Reading – 30 minutes per day. Mathematical study on the brilliant.org site 20 minutes per day – check it out! Piano – 30 minutes per day. I meditate for a minimum of 10 minutes daily so I am left with 20 minutes for extra cognitive work which may be extra reading or meditation, Audible listening, pretty much wherever my mind wants to go for the day.

## Relationships: 10% daily

I am focused on spending just under 2.5hrs per day developing and improving my immediate relationships, and then outwards from there.

This will include, let's say, an evening spent with my wife watching some TV (usually in Spanish but I don't count it as cognitive!) and chatting for an hour as part of this but preferably it is close interaction time such as playing with my son or being with my wife without background distractions. I will also include conversations with friends and other family members that are developmental to this time rather than just face-to-face communication.

## Work: 30% daily

While this is not one of the category headings in KongDay, it is essential to understand how much of your daily % is spent working. This percentage means I cap my work at just over 7hrs daily otherwise my other life areas will suffer. On many days I will work fewer hours than this, giving me more time to work further on other categories. However, I don't flex it to the extent of working, say, 9 hours one day knowing I will have only 5hrs of work the next day. That could lead to the system soon falling apart. 1-2 days of the week I find myself working 12-13hr days with commitments. I still try and find time during this work, no mater how small, to check off some of my KongDay tasks.

## Daily fixed: 6%

Again, an extra factor, almost 1.5 hrs, purely to allow leeway for essentials such as brushing teeth, showering, eating meals and random internet browsing such as social media (often at the midday to 1pm slot, which works for me).

This is my remaining time allowance on top of the previous allocation. Of course, some days I may work less so have more extra percentages to use, but for my scoring I must hit these breakdown minimums to be in the 5-scoring category. Anything less cannot be a 5 and will end up being somewhere between 1 and 4.

# It only works if you work it

So, that is the premise of the scoring system, which has proven to be successful with many of the people I have worked with. I feel it is easy to implement and you can be the judge of how the concept changes your life.

*Does it always work?*

Well, my system and work of course, like life, has seen many failures, but understanding the key reason for those failures is important. It would be easy for me to claim that every person adopting KongDay has seen their life transformed. However, the truth is that some people never really buy into the methodology for themselves. They feel that things will only change if someone can be there to implement the program for them and guide them every step of the way. This is not life and not how KongDay works! It is a framework for living a healthy, balanced and fulfilled life, but it is essential that you take charge. You do not need me or anyone else to be at your side. Take lessons from others who suggest something to try and then go forth. Only you can instigate and monitor your every action. I merely hope I have opened a mindset shift for you to start.

I have had occasions where I have had to accept that I or the system could not help. For instance, I spent 3 years working with a man who could not get his weight down to body fat goals (one of the easiest areas to achieve in KongDay with system buy in). We tried multiple different nutrition interventions and even other coaches to try to achieve his targets yet consistently failed. I became frustrated at his constant ability to produce a reason why the numerical target was not being hit, and in the end, I had to ask the client to stop working with me. No matter what I tried I could not produce the result he wanted so in the end I could not keep accepting the consulting fees. I feel that his failure was his honesty to his actions. His mindset became an immovable problem, but I am hopeful that one day he will break free and understand that an honest self-assessment is, although hard in the short term, healthy in the long term for change.

Another example would be a client who flew through the system and really changed his desires and life around. The problem with this is his wife did not like the different person he became. The relationship ended in a divorce and for a while I was troubled as being the potential key cause. In reflection the change might suggest that like many couples, the future pushes them apart. We become different people and a reality of constant change means our life will change. The client still works with me and seems happier and content with the current progress of his life.

> *The need for honesty, with yourself and those helping you on your journey, is critical. Even if the dog did eat your homework. It's still not there.*

The 1-5 KongDay scoring system for each factor is your own daily assessment of how you have performed that day against your goals. In many cases it is a qualitative score rather than a quantitative one, which requires you to be as objective as possible within such an assessment framework. If you are going to succumb to bias, be hard on yourself rather than too easy on yourself! In that way you can only over-perform rather than underachieve.

Denis Waitley an American motivation speaker who wrote *The Psychology of Winning* said it best:

> **"The primary success factor is knowing how to learn from others and rely on yourself."**
>
> Denis Waitley

No matter what I have said in this book, it is you who must use the ideas behind this system to make your life better. If you feel areas need to be changed and adapted that is absolutely fine if you can justify the results.

*But I promise you, if you are honest with yourself throughout, it will work!*

# 9: STARTING YOUR KONGDAY JOURNEY

NOW THAT YOU have read in detail about each of the 5 KongDay categories and combined these with the vital 6th aspect of coordinating them in balance with each other, here is my guide on how to start implementing KongDay to improve your life... from today.

I referred to Victor Frankl in Chapter 4, and his system titled logotherapy which embraced the idea of suffering as crucial to navigating life. His book title, *Man's Search for Meaning*, hammers home the reality that the very tenet that causes most people to become forlorn about their life is the mental state they foster. I have found that asking people what meaning they live for often causes people to view their life as insignificant because they view their current work as unimportant. Unless you perform life-changing charity or social work it is often easy to view your time as meaningless, creating an empty feeling inside of futility. What difference would it make if I was not here, who will remember me when I am gone, etc. Frankl wanted to stress that killing yourself was a regular and real occurrence in the Nazi concentration camps because life no longer had meaning. His system found a way to create meaning to stay alive and I believe once you start scoring your life in the 6 areas you will also start to find a simple meaning for living better.

We all need a system that acts as a practical tool to combat suffering. Of course, no one reading this book is suffering to anything like the level that Frankl describes, but boredom and filling time with the wrong activities (all too easy in today's online world) will lead the brain down a path that moves an individual away from achieving a balanced mind. Dedicating time every day to the key areas I have outlined will reinforce your ability to fight depression and a problematic mind. You suddenly also have a clear purpose and meaning to improve 6 areas of your life, every day.

If you are serious about scoring your progress, then there are two ways to approach this. To get you started, on the final page of this book is a blank template for you to use to create your own score charts for monitoring daily the 6 key areas. The first way is to record progress electronically on a PC or on your phone. This is preferable, as it is quicker, easier, always accessible and you can add colour to the chart as I have done in the examples in this book. To create the template version in Excel only took me a few minutes, and once you've created a master version, it's easy to personalise sheets for each of the 6 categories you should be monitoring - physicality, nutrition, cognition, sleep, relationships. The second way is to photocopy this template and create paper versions which you then fill in daily for the month of scoring.

You don't need to wait until 1st January to start this! Feel free to start mid-way through a calendar year. Even from, say, September/October onwards, you will start to see a pattern of progress across a few months.

If you do none of the scoring, please at least begin with the 4 simple habits below. When performed daily these will at the very least go a long way to satisfying your experience.

They are:

1. **JOURNALLING** – Write about your day and what comes to mind when you review it. This can be often as short as 5 minutes at the end of each day.
2. **MEDITATION** – Just give yourself 5-10 minutes daily to be in silence and listen to your breathing. Use expert guidance to help you when you start.
3. **TRACKING YOUR HRV** – This is quick and easy. Use a tracker tool to register your heart beats and monitor the daily changes.
4. **READING** – Even reading for short periods daily will change your mindset and experience like no other medium. Do this every day and start to see the effect.

Once you fully absorb these habits into your life you will see how the feelings and problematic emotions in life still exist, but they are no longer amplified as they are when you align your meaning to goals of money, power or the ego. No one can do anything to fully stop problems and issues existing both in society and your mind, but we can manage the input.

As we have outlined throughout this book, the only successful approach is to get up every single day and perform habits that shut down negativity. Your feedback mechanism then becomes a process that is driving your life. I will also list a 3-area daily focus that you can use to simplify your starting journey:

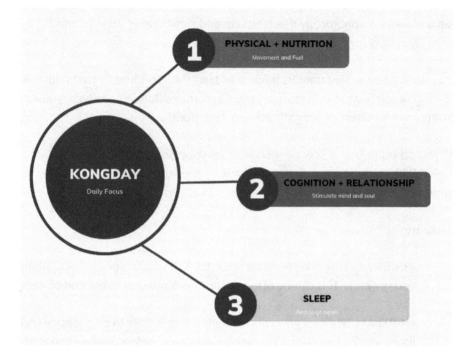

Whatever it is, force yourself to conduct some physical movement every single day. Nutrition is an extension to this area and you will have step 1 completed. Step 2 asks you to stimulate your mind by performing cognitive tasks and navigating your current relationship actions. Step 3 is the icing on the cake and places emphasis on getting a good night's sleep. This is to firstly consolidate the work performed today and importantly to be ready to go again tomorrow on this same attack.

Using this methodology helps to silence the brain. It is easier to do this in some areas more than others, but you owe it to yourself to work on yourself. This is the daily goal. You will create success across the board and produce daily data that tells you where you have excelled and where you need to do better. I truly hope that you can find success in using a personalised accountability system that you create and review. This is what I have learnt from some of the greatest performance coaches over decades. You cannot spend all your todays trying to live completely in only that moment because you will suffer later. You need to live for the moment (as we are always told) but you need to use a daily system for how – KongDay can be that system. Your scoring of yesterday is not relevant to today's score, but it is important for your compounding. Further you can strive daily to beat yesterdays score. Monitoring charts and personal data should become addictive. Playing games is fun.

*Make your life analysis fun and reap the benefit.*

The continuity you can create in your scores is worth more than any financial investment prosperity. This is your life and it's getting shorter every single day.

Now get out there and get after it, as the clock has never stopped ticking.

# Your KongDay score sheet

Use the chart opposite to map your scores. Enter the month and year as the chart title (e.g. January 2023). Enter your scores for each category in the corresponding day of the month. Calculate your averages at the bottom by adding up the scores for the days and dividing that figure by the total number of days.

Month/Year: _____

| Day | Sleep | Nutrition | Physical | Cognitive | Relationships | Balance | Total |
|---|---|---|---|---|---|---|---|
| 1 | | | | | | | |
| 2 | | | | | | | |
| 3 | | | | | | | |
| 4 | | | | | | | |
| 5 | | | | | | | |
| 6 | | | | | | | |
| 7 | | | | | | | |
| 8 | | | | | | | |
| 9 | | | | | | | |
| 10 | | | | | | | |
| 11 | | | | | | | |
| 12 | | | | | | | |
| 13 | | | | | | | |
| 14 | | | | | | | |
| 15 | | | | | | | |
| 16 | | | | | | | |
| 17 | | | | | | | |
| 18 | | | | | | | |
| 19 | | | | | | | |
| 20 | | | | | | | |
| 21 | | | | | | | |
| 22 | | | | | | | |
| 23 | | | | | | | |
| 24 | | | | | | | |
| 25 | | | | | | | |
| 26 | | | | | | | |
| 27 | | | | | | | |
| 28 | | | | | | | |
| 29 | | | | | | | |
| 30 | | | | | | | |
| 31 | | | | | | | |

KONGDAY: Quantifying your life to success

CPSIA information can be obtained
at www.ICGtesting.com
Printed in the USA
BVHW051531130123
656256BV00011B/376